Developing the Child with Down's Syndrome

Resources in Education

Resources in Education

Developing the Child with Down's Syndrome

A Guide for Teachers, Parents and Carers

Joyce Mepsted

Northcote House

© Copyright 1998 by Joyce Mepsted

First published in 1988 as *Your Child Needs You.*
Second edition (revised and rewritten) published in 1998
by Northcote House Publishers Ltd, Plymbridge House,
Estover Road, Plymouth PL6 7PY, United Kingdom.
Tel: Plymouth (01752) 202368. Fax: (01752) 202330.

ISBN 0-7463-06865

Typeset by Kestrel Data, Exeter
Printed and bound in Great Britain

To Viv Tonkin, who encouraged me to write,
and to all the parents who have expressed a need for
this book and who have continued to give me support
and encouragement.

Contents

Heaven's Very Special Child

A meeting was held quite far from earth
'It's time again for another birth,'
Said the Angels to the Lord above,
'This special child will need much love,
His progress may seem very slow,
Accomplishments he may not show
And he'll require extra care
From the folks he meets way down there.
He may not run or laugh or play
His thoughts may seem quite far away,
In many ways he won't adapt
And he'll be known as handicapped.
So let's be careful where he's sent
We want his life to be content.
Please, Lord, find the parents who
Will do a special job for you.
They will not realise right away
The leading role they're asked to play,
But with this child sent from above
Come stronger faith and richer love.
And soon they'll know the privilege given
In caring for this gift from heaven.
Their precious child so meek and mild
Is "Heaven's very special child".'

Author unknown

Foreword

In the course of the past thirty or forty years, a quiet revolution has been taking place regarding the developmental and educational prospects of children with Down's Syndrome, a revolution still partly unknown to new parents and even to some professionals.

When my own work began in 1959, most children with Down's Syndrome were believed to be severely mentally handicapped. The first inkling that this might *not* always be so came from a book by Nigel Hunt, the first Down's Syndrome author, and from the developmental work of Dr Lydia de Coriat in South America.

At that time, children with Down's Syndrome usually spent their often short lives in institutions and many more spent their adult lives behind their forbidding walls. Life expectancy was low; many did not even reach their first birthday, fewer still their fifth. The development of antibiotics, cardiac surgery and improved home conditions, nutrition and central heating have largely curbed this early mortality, and most can now look forward to a reasonable life span.

However, until 1970 no child with Down's Syndrome had a legal right to attend any form of school; only a lucky minority attended Junior Training Centres where staff, often ill-trained and ill-paid, made heroic efforts to give them basic social training inside draughty and depressing church halls.

Since my own introduction of the idea of Early Intervention into this country, however, the sky has gradually lightened; pressure from parents, from the Down's Syndrome Association and from enlightened professionals has led to a groundswell of discontent with the old order. The successive Education Acts of the 1970s and 1980s and the influence of the *Warnock Report* opened the door to education in schools for the severely subnormal and for children with Down's Syndrome. It was not long before children with Down's Syndrome were showing that they could benefit from education alongside children with Mild Learning Difficulties, and since the 1981 Education Act (and

11

even be   ny were becoming fully integrated into ordinary
schools

A sample survey in 1981 by the National Centre showed that nearly
a quarter of the children who had followed our developmental
programmes were already in normal infant, junior and secondary
schools; one-third were in schools for children with Mild Learning
Difficulties, and a decreasing minority in schools for those with Severe
Learning Difficulties, though towards the upper end of that category.
The whole wide range of ability has moved upwards to a substantial
degree. With ever-greater sophistication in early treatment and
training, many more in the future are likely to be placed in the mildly
retarded category. Meanwhile steady progress in genetics and genetic
biochemistry has even suggested a distant prospect of correction of the
condition.

But every step depends upon the attitudes of society. Parents,
teachers, doctors, researchers and the general public each have their
part to play. To succeed with the child with Down's Syndrome requires
a positive act of faith from parents and a great deal of hard work,
especially in the crucial early years, and Joyce Mepsted's book reflects
her research into attitudes. The whole book is heartening, practical and
comforting guide to our children's needs, and will change the early
despair of many parents into resolution and optimism. Her own long
experience in Special Education is reflected in the excellent chapters
on education in the home and at school. She gives valuable advice on
the development of learning skills and on the social development so
crucial if our children are to take their full place as accepted and valued
members of the general community.

One of the keys to this work is Mrs Mepsted's stress on the avoidance
of the old self-fulfilling prophecies which did so much harm in the past.
As she emphasises, children respond to expectation and the parent who
expects change and development is well on the way towards bringing
it about.

Mrs Mepsted's book blows a breath of fresh air into an area where
in many professional studies all is gloom. One of the delightful aspects
of her book are the many happy examples she gives, from her
professional experience as a teacher of children with learning disabilities, of success and achievement by the children. On every page,
too, her own devotion to her work and to the children shines through
as a reflection of the happiness she feels for their achievements.
Whether she deals with the child as a member of the family, as a
schoolchild or as a social being, what comes through always is the real
joy that comes from working with children with Down's Syndrome,

most of whom in my own long experience of children from over forty countries are very cheerful beings. Above all children with Down's Syndrome learn by social mimicry, and it is up to us to provide them with the right models. 'Building' one's own child is always a fascinating job, if rightly approached; building a child for whom the future at first looks dark and for whom many of the instructions are missing is an even more satisfying achievement. My own two children with learning disabilities have long convinced me of that.

This book will give to many parents the resolution to achieve their objectives and Mrs Mepsted's many useful tips, drawn from deep professional experience, will go a long way towards the goal. Above all, however, this is a happy and supportive book which will hopefully change many negative attitudes among parents and professionals alike, many of whom may be still dogged by the myths and case histories of former institutional cases. Mrs Mepsted sees the child with Down's Syndrome first and foremost as an individual child rather than as a representative of a disabling condition, and guides the parent, as well as those with care and responsibility, towards a thoroughly positive view which will go a long way towards making him a child with a future. I would say that this book is a must for all new parents, teachers and carers, and for those parents of older children whose early view of the condition has been a depressed and dispiriting one. It replaces despair with purpose.

Rex Brinkworth MBE BA CertEd DCP
Hon. Director, National Centre for Down's Syndrome.
Founder, Down's Syndrome Association
Retired Senior Lecturer in Psychology and Special Education,
University of Central England, Birmingham.

Introduction

I have been a teacher in Special Education happily involved with children with learning disabilities for many years and more recently have worked with teachers and carers having responsibility for children with Down's Syndrome. On taking up a new appointment as teacher in charge of a new Special Unit for children with severe learning difficulties, attached to a mainstream primary school, I found myself within the first twelve months responsible for the education and welfare of four young children with Down's Syndrome, then aged four to five and a half. In addition I have known and worked with children with Down's Syndrome up to eighteen years of age.

Through talking to the parents, teachers and carers and discussing the problems they had faced we realised there was a need for an informative book to provide a means of help and support, particularly in the early days for parents with a new baby with Down's Syndrome. Many in particular expressed the need for a book which would be thoroughly (and rightly) positive in outlook. This book, it is hoped, will fulfil this need.

Lack of knowledge and experience

Parents whose new baby has Down's Syndrome seldom have any knowledge or experience of what to expect. They are told that their child has an 'extra chromosome' and is 'mentally handicapped' or has learning disabilities. Often those whose help and advice they seek – even family doctors, health visitors or social workers – have themselves little or no previous experience of this condition and the new parents return home to face an unknown future with their baby. Help and advice *is* available, but more often than not proves difficult to find.

Again it has been found, all too frequently, that well-meaning but ill-informed friends will say that these children are 'always happy and loving', or that 'they will never be able to do anything'. Kind or hurtful? Certainly not very helpful, for don't we *all* wish our children to be happy and loving? Likewise all children can certainly do something, depending not only on their ability but on the opportunities open to them, and the quality of their environment.

Every child's birthright
First, and most important of all, we should consider the child himself. Each child, whether experiencing learning difficulties or not, has his or her own birthright. He is a unique member of the human race, like any one of us, with his own personality, inherited characteristics, and abilities. He has likes and dislikes and feelings of his own, no different from the rest of us. All children have the same basic needs of love and security, food, warmth, clothing and interesting things to do, within a warm and caring home atmosphere and environment.

At one time it was generally assumed that children with Down's Syndrome would, indeed, never learn anything! More recently it has been thought that they could be taught certain skills – but could never learn naturally or by copying others. Let me say now – *give them the opportunity to try!* This, I feel, has so often been denied them, and you may be quite surprised at just how much your child with Down's Syndrome will achieve. Naturally, within this group of children, as within any other group, there will be a wide range of ability and aptitude. But any step forward, however small, is a vital one for these children; they too can derive so much pleasure, confidence and self-esteem from the knowledge that they can do things for themselves and attain a worthwhile measure of independence and responsibility.

They may develop more slowly than other children and not become responsible for themselves at such an early age; but their general pattern of progress and development will certainly follow that of their brothers and sisters. The steps along the way may be smaller, but are equally, and in many instances, more rewarding. They, too, need help and encouragement – and praise! Indeed they have every right to demand and expect more help and support than their so-called 'normal' brothers and sisters in fulfilling their potential, for their needs are greater. Given the right opportunity many continue to develop and mature beyond the usual school-leaving age. Many local authorities and colleges now recognise this potential and in some areas post-sixteen provision for both educational and social development is becoming increasingly available.

New attitudes
In recent years much more attention has been paid to the problems related to learning disability and the general public too has become

more aware. There is less stigma attached to this condition than once there was. The fact that these individuals are coming to take their place in the community, and recognised and accepted as such, even from an early age, must surely do much to further their cause, instead of being kept hidden and being put away from society. In my experience, once a child with a disability has been accepted and is known as an individual in his or her own right the initial reaction and aversion to the condition as such has been overcome; they are then rightly accepted for *who* they are, and not what they are.

Before starting school, one of my pupils used to accompany his mother on regular shopping expeditions to the local shops. His absence on one occasion was missed by one lady shopkeeper who asked where he was. 'Oh, he's started school,' said mum. 'Has he?' said the shopkeeper, 'which one?' To which the mother proudly replied that he now attended the Special Unit at the local primary school. The embarrassed shopkeeper was covered with confusion as she admitted that she had not even realised that the child had a learning disability.

These days, fortunately, much more is being done to help these young people to integrate into the community. The different professions involved provide a multi-disciplinary team able to offer a good deal of support and resources. By working together these various professions – education, medical, psychological, social services and voluntary agencies – can contribute towards a more positive future. In the present climate of public opinion, through the dedicated work of the people involved, and with the resources now being made available, conditions can only improve to help our children to fulfil their lives, and so become as far as possible useful, independent and responsible members of society. Increasingly more and more children with Down's Syndrome are being educated full time within the mainstream, with an entitlement to the National Curriculum. The children with Down's Syndrome that I am fortunate to know and work with are really a pleasure and delight to be with. They arrive in the morning full of bounce and enthusiasm which continues throughout the shared activities of the day. Learning is fun and very rewarding! I see their development and education as a team effort, with all agencies involved, including the parents. All have an important role in helping these children meet their individual needs.

The children's overall development is assessed within five major areas. These concern:

- the acquisition of self-help skills
- social competence

17

- physical development (which covers both fine and gross motor co-ordination)
- communication skills
- cognitive – academic – development.

Throughout their pre-school and school life consideration is given to their all-round development and well-being. We look on the child as a whole person.

The children in my own Unit have really surprised and pleased me by their progress and achievement in their first year at school. However, the teacher cannot take all the credit; had it not been for the backing and support of other professionals, and the stimulation and dedication of the parents, much less would have been achieved. We must not forget, either, that it is the children themselves who have succeeded so far and whom this is all about. Without their own natural enthusiasm and lively interest none of us would have succeeded at all. They have provided the inspiration to write this book and have made it possible. With love, encouragement and support all children with Down's Syndrome will learn to participate and become valued members of their family, school and community.

As these children grow up in the modern world, we can only hope, in this more enlightened age, that more provision will be made to meet their particular needs. In many places excellent resources are available, and the children can fulfil themselves throughout their school lives and beyond. They have a chance now to become valuable members of our society, taking their place with the rest of us, and able to make their own unique contribution and lead full and happy lives.

Children with Down's Syndrome can learn and do learn. They can be lively, active and interested children – just give them the opportunity to try, and you will be amazed how well they will respond. I have learned so much from the children themselves – they are continually showing me that they can – and will! They are, indeed, very special children with very special needs – to which you as teachers, parents or carers are in a unique position to respond.

Please note!
To avoid clumsy expression (him/her, his/hers, etc.) and for ease of reading, the child is frequently referred to as 'he' or 'him', whether male or female, and no discourtesy or bias is intended.

1
Fear and Prejudice: The New Baby

Mixed feelings: rejection and acceptance

A new baby! Congratulations are in order! Initial reactions to having a baby with Down's Syndrome are many and varied, which is quite natural; they can range anywhere between complete rejection and total acceptance, often wavering between the two. Coming to terms with the fact that a new baby has Down's Syndrome is a whole-family experience and one which the parents need to face together. Adults as well as children are individuals, and have their own different needs. Some prefer to talk the matter over with their doctor or social worker, hopefully one with knowledge and expertise in this field. Others are anxious to meet other families with a baby or child with Down's Syndrome, to share their experiences and talk about what it will be like to rear their baby, and to see what other children are like. Such contacts can be arranged through the paediatrician, health visitor or social worker.

Most parents have little or no previous knowledge or experience of this condition. During pregnancy parents often wonder if the child the mother is carrying will have anything 'wrong' with it, and naturally enough hope to produce a 'normal' baby. The arrival of a baby with Down's Syndrome is frequently distressing and conflicting feelings and emotions are experienced, even feelings of guilt and blame. But you are *not* to blame if your baby is different. It was something you had no control over, since it happened at conception.

No child is born absolutely perfect! Surprisingly, perhaps, many disabilities can occur at conception, during pregnancy, at birth, or during the first few days following the birth (the perinatal period). And after all we can all suffer an accident or infection at any time which could result in some disabling condition. At least you have the benefit of knowledge and understanding of what makes this baby an individual from the start.

How the news is broken to the parents can vary enormously. Some mothers realise almost immediately that there is something different about their baby, either instinctively or by sensing a difference in attitude or attention from the medical staff however unintentional. In some cases even the hospital staff can be slow to notice the fact, since it is not always immediately apparent. How and when the parents are told can present something of a problem to the doctors and medical staff. It is not easy to explain to proud new parents that their long-awaited baby is different from the other babies in the ward, and how and why it is not the same. Doctors usually prefer to break the news to both parents together, and ideally after they have both seen and held the child. They are then discussing *this* baby and its condition, and not an unknown baby in another room.

Down's Syndrome is usually first diagnosed by noting the physical features present – the mongoloid features and flattish faces, slanty eyes and high cheekbones, large tongue, single palm-crease, floppy limbs and difficulty in sucking. Some or all of these conditions may be present. To confirm this a small blood sample is taken from the baby in order to make a chromosome count, as all chromosomes are present in each cell of the body. This test is relatively quick and easy to perform; it does not take long before the results are through.

Another problem to be faced is what to tell the grandparents, family and friends. This can result in a mixed reception too, producing a variety of feelings and preconceived ideas. You will probably find that the sooner it is done, the sooner they will accept it. Even if you find it hard at first the straightforward honest approach is best in the long run. But you know your family and friends best and how to approach them. Generally speaking, family and friends can be helpful and supportive, especially the ones more enlightened about the problems of learning disabilities. It is often the older generation who find it hardest to accept. Ignorance of the facts and fear of the unknown together with lack of any previous experience may result in people showing fear and prejudice.

'Why should this happen to me?' 'What have we done to deserve this?' Such sentiments must be felt by many new parents presented with some unusual condition or disability in their child. 'Why *should* my baby be different?' At first, feelings of rejection are very natural. You will find that nearly all parents experience this. They may not want to know the baby or have anything to do with him.

'We were stunned.' 'I was horrified.' 'You hear of it happening to other people.' These are some of the immediate responses from new parents. Others feel that they want to get rid of the baby, perhaps put it in a home and forget about it. But then, 'I took one look at my baby and I realised how much he needed me,' one mother told me; 'I felt protective towards him.' All new babies have very special needs. Caring for these needs – comforting, feeding, bathing, dressing and playing – form that basis of a good and happy relationship to which the child himself will respond and feel secure and happy. Give him plenty of love and cuddles. From here on he can be treated just like any 'other' baby!

Parents can experience a fear of the unknown or the future as well as the usual prejudices against anything which may appear abnormal or imperfect – even a horror or revulsion against anything not 'normal', perfect or acceptable. These feelings are quite natural and need to be faced before an adjustment can be made. All parents vary in the way they are able to handle and resolve the situation. Indeed some do reject the baby totally. Many feel despair for their child and the future. There can be very few who are able to accept the child fully when the condition is first explained. Both the father and the mother need time – time to talk over their feelings, hopes and expectations. Counselling may be available but in the end it is their decision and their choice alone.

Difficulties can appear insurmountable, especially if faced alone. But doesn't life in general have its ups and downs, problems and pitfalls, as well as success and rewards? Accidents and disasters of all kinds can occur at any time.

A lot of parents have been helped at this time by meeting other children with Down's Syndrome at home or at toddler groups (contact your health visitor or social worker) and seeing for themselves that they are just children with their own personalities and abilities. They can also see for themselves that they are able to walk, talk, play and respond – just like any other child. They are also able to understand that their baby is special. The child will need a lot of care and attention to help him grow. The responsibility is theirs and the child needs their love and care to be able grow up happy and confident.

Sometimes the decision may be to treat the child as normal from the start, and so expect him to behave and to do things like anyone else. Older people with Down's Syndrome can become reasonably in-dependent and responsible. They can do things for themselves: shop, cook, catch a bus or attend a youth club. Bringing up any baby is not easy, but bringing up a baby with Down's Syndrome successfully can be hard work. Difficulties can be overcome, and hard work usually results in achievement. The rewards may not be reaped until later, but as a family you will all share in the benefits.

The clinical condition

What *is* Down's Syndrome and how is it caused? A brief outline will be given at this point (a more detailed explanation is given in Appendix I). The answer really is quite simple. Basically it means that the baby has an extra chromosome present in the cells of the body, and there may be some degree of learning disability. He would not then be described as *physically* handicapped since there may be no actual physical disability present. Neither can he be described as *physiologically* handicapped, since there may be no noticeable impairment or malformation of his bodily actions or functions. Rather, I would describe the condition as a *genetic* handicap, since the abnormality is contained within his genetic make-up. This is a result of an unusual division of the chromosomes which occurs from the moment the original fertilised egg begins to divide and grow. This is called trisomy 21; it results in three number 21 chromosomes being present in the cell whereas the rest of the 23 chromosomes are in pairs, one set of each being inherited from each parent.

The diagnosis will normally be confirmed by taking a small blood sample and making a chromosome count. Medical science can now explain *how* this happens but not yet *why*.

This syndrome results in certain features and characteristics being commonly shared and recognised in children with Down's Syndrome. But putting these aside, it is only fair to regard the child as an individual personality in his own right. Like the rest of us, the child will inherit characteristics from both sides of the family.

General development depends so much on the secure, stimulating and happy environment in which the child is brought up. Enjoy your baby. It is yours. Help him to develop in his own way and take pleasure in sharing his successes. You will be surprised to discover what your child is capable of. One mother said to me, 'Had I known what children with Down's Syndrome were like I would never have asked for an amniocentesis when I was pregnant.' (Her own daughter has hydrocephalus with complications!)

Associated problems

You may well find that your child has additional complications, to a greater or lesser degree, depending on the individual. But, remember that few babies pass through babyhood without some ailment or other! Children with Down's Syndrome are often prone to chest infections, colds, catarrh and runny noses. Some, too, have sticky eyes which need to be bathed regularly. This can be due to blocked tear ducts.

Their general health has to be watched closely. Many suffer from catarrh, and a blocked-up stuffy feeling may contribute towards lethargy or listlessness. Catarrh and associated blocked tubes may produce sinus problems, speech or adenoid problems, or cause a slight hearing loss. Adenoids may be removed if your child has a difficulty and their removal at a later date may improve his speech.

Similarly if he has a slight fluctuating hearing loss your specialist may suggest draining the tubes and fitting a gromet. This should improve the hearing and is only a temporary inconvenience; but, again, at a later stage many children have this problem, too. The gromet is a small cone-shaped object fitted in the ear drum. As the skin heals it pushes the gromet out, usually over a few months.

Constant colds can lodge on the chest and result in infection or difficulty in breathing, especially at night. With the thorough medical examination given to these children a slight heart murmur is sometimes found. If only slight it would not have been noticed in an otherwise healthy baby and is sometimes outgrown by the time the child starts school.

Another feature common to most of the children is a rather larger thickened tongue. This is not improved as the children grow older if they are not told to put it back in the mouth. Exposure to the air will encourage it to become dry and possibly bigger! Often the jaw and facial muscles are slack and lack tone. These together can result in speech difficulties and loss of clarity in speech – even if they are, in fact, producing the correct sounds in the throat. Clear articulation depends on adequate reproduction through the mouth, tongue, teeth and lips and the fact that they in turn are working properly. In this instance the tip of the tongue, teeth and lips will improve by stimulation. Encourage the child to lick lollies, suck through straws, blow bubbles and brush the teeth (and the tip of the tongue) – all enjoyable activities!

This general lack of muscle tone, floppiness, seems to affect not only the mouth. If the arms and legs lack muscle tone, too, the baby will feel very 'floppy'. However, a lively active baby will be busy exercising his own limbs and muscles – and soon making up for this defect! If your baby is quieter, less active or lazy you may feel that you wish to exercise with him. This too can be enjoyable as a shared experience. A baby needs to become aware of his own body and able to explore the space around him. Just watch the pleasure on a baby's face when he is able to kick, stretch and twist his own body and push himself around on the floor. If you feel that you need more expert advice in this area, just ask for a copy of the booklet *Your Baby Has Down's Syndrome* available from The Down's Syndrome Association, it will give you plenty of ideas and information.

The parents are the ones who know their baby best. They will be able to tell if he is well and happy, if he is taking an interest in his surroundings and responding to them. Should you feel that he is suffering, or unable to take an interest in things that you are doing with him and generally not responding, do go and have a chat with your own doctor or paediatrician. The welfare of your child is their responsibility, too. They are there to help and can put you in touch with a specialist if necessary. Similarly if you have regular visits from your health visitor or social worker at this stage they too are well placed to offer help and advice or put you in touch with someone else who will be able to assist.

Development during infancy

What can a baby do by the time he is between six and twelve months old? Quite a lot really! He starts to learn about himself and his surroundings from the moment he is born, and should respond to plenty of encouragement. Contrary to the old popular belief, babies are surprisingly alert and instinctively aware of things going on around them. They learn and develop all the time. Enjoy your baby – he will respond to your efforts. Take pleasure in caring for him; play with him, give him time and attention. Let him have interesting things to watch when he is lying in his cot or pram – bright colours, moving objects, different sounds. Prop him up where he can watch his immediate world revolve around him, and where he can watch you too. Talk to him and sing. Offer him a variety of things to make life continually interesting and stimulating. Encourage him to explore his own body and things around him by giving him things to touch and hold, and, as he gets older, to push and pull.

Your baby may be slower to do things but each little step forward will be a big achievement for him – and for you too! Try to give praise continually, encourage and reward with words, smiles and cuddles. Touching your baby and handling him is very important for you both: it helps to build the bond between you. This means fathers too! Your baby is part of your family and that means working together. Your baby needs to feel happy and secure. He needs you both and needs to know in return that he too is loved and needed. All babies respond to feelings and can be just as sensitive as you are. You may feel despondent if you get no response at first, but don't give up, keep on trying. Your baby's happiness and well-being is well worth the effort.

Most parents have a natural tendency to compare their child with others, and, of course, take pride in their development and acquisition of skills. Don't worry too much if you find that your baby is slower than others. Follow the steps of normal child development and use them as guidelines, and just adapt the pace to suit your child. Remember that your child is an individual; measure his progress within his own development and how well he himself is doing.

Many babies with Down's Syndrome can perform to a level comparable to their own age group if given sufficient attention and stimulation from the start. This should continue into the toddler stage and up to the time they are ready for school. Three-year-old children are able to play with toys, build with bricks, stack play cups, enjoy picture books, listen to stories and talk about the pictures. They know nursery rhymes and action songs, and will listen to adult talk and vocalise themselves. They play with their own toys happily alongside or with other children and join in group games, and enjoy scribbling with chalk and crayons. They like helping mummy and will accompany her in jobs around the house.

These are some of the things to aim for. You can probably think of many more. First and foremost treat your baby and toddler as a normal child. He *is* a child first and foremost; the learning disability is of secondary importance which you can take account of, but do not make *too* many allowances or excuses for it. You will not want to hold him back. Push him forward and provide a variety of experiences so that he can try to be as socially competent as his friends. Let him try to do things for himself and help with his own dressing, undressing, going to the toilet, washing and feeding himself.

Offer your child plenty of opportunities. Show him you are happy and pleased with his efforts. You will find it rewarding for all of you. They cannot learn if you do not show them. Your children will only learn how to do things if you can give them the time and the patience to show them how. Make life interesting, too. Plan trips and shopping expeditions and take them with you. These activities can provide a wealth of new experiences for you to share together.

Talk about what you can see and what you are doing. The acquisition of language skills is an important part of every child's development, and essential to the ability to communicate. Overall language development involves listening to the spoken word, and the ability to hold onto the sequence. The child then has to be able to organise this information from his previous experiences and understanding of the meaning, and finally to respond and vocalise himself. Try to develop his general understanding and awareness.

You can also encourage an interest in books. There are plenty of good children's books in print these days that contain good stories, beautiful pictures and things to do. Look for some books that have peep-holes in the pages, flaps to lift and tabs to pull so that the characters move. Talk about the story and the pictures. Encourage your child to point out different things in the picture and talk about colours, numbers, shapes and sizes. Even if your child has difficulty in talking or can't express himself very clearly, an ability to understand the spoken word will greatly assist his language development, and enable him to relate to his surroundings and to people and places around him. Explore your local bookshop and children's library.

Sources of help and support
You will obviously want to know how your baby is progressing and what sort of things children of a similar age can do. It it gratifying, too, to be complimented on your own child's progress and skills. It is natural for most parents to want to compare their own child's development with that of other children. Actually, this is something which I try very hard as a teacher *not* to do when talking to parents – to compare one child's development or progress with another, the group, or even with so-called 'normal' development. Parents, however, do ask this question seeking assurance that their child is developing along regular patterns of growth and behaviour.

In general conversation, it is very hard to discuss a particular group of children without making comparisons. Many new parents, as well as those with young children with Down's Syndrome, often derive comfort from such discussions. It is indeed helpful to discover when your baby of twelve months shows absolutely no sign of walking – or even yet of crawling (and you are beginning to wonder if he ever will!) that the lively three-year-old across the room did not start walking until the age of two, and what's more did not even crawl first! It only goes to prove that all children are different and develop at their own pace. Such discussions with other parents can provide hope and comfort and provide a positive feedback. This is especially so when you may feel that you are battling along on your own and seeing no signs of progress – no way out of the wood! It certainly helps, too, to find that you are not isolated, or working in the dark on your own, or that you are the only ones with these particular problems to handle.

Parents of children with Down's Syndrome can join a local group of the Down's Syndrome Association or a local branch of Mencap; members can share their experiences, deriving benefit from mutual help and support. They have plenty in common to discuss, and need not feel so lonely when they discover that other parents have just the same problems! Experiences can be recognised and shared – the ups and downs of family life, as well as the rewards, pleasures and disappointments, the smiles and tears. All these are encountered when rearing children.

Social and group activities are arranged which cater for the needs of the parents as well as those of the children. After all, we all need a break from time to time and the chance to relax and enjoy ourselves (even if we are talking shop!). This also provides an opportunity to 'recharge the batteries' before returning afresh to the daily task of managing a child with special needs – hard work, certainly, but very rewarding and often great fun. A sense of humour helps immensely. In fact, I would say that it is an essential prerequisite! How often have I heard people say, 'If I didn't laugh about it I'd cry!'

Common experiences are well worth sharing – the good as well as the not-so-good. There are bound to be a lot of similarities, and now you will want to look more closely at more general and normal patterns of growth and development.

When you take your baby for regular check-ups at the baby clinic the doctor, nurse and health visitor – whom you will have met already – can assure you that he is making progress and developing satisfactorily at his own pace. A check, too, can be kept on his general health. Do make a point of asking advice, and bring up any questions or problems on which you would like help or guidance. These people are here to help you. If you don't get a satisfactory answer then never be afraid to ask where you can get more information. Don't be disappointed if your baby is not progressing as quickly as other children of a similar age seem to be – he will naturally need more time to be shown and encouraged to move around, to look at things and handle objects. Also he will need more time to practise and acquire new skills, to establish a pattern of learning and become more proficient. You may find it useful to read one or two general books on infant and child development. Have a look around a good book shop or make enquiries at your local library. Library services are available in all areas – including a mobile library if you live in an isolated rural area – and the staff can be very friendly and helpful. They can look out books for you and obtain or reserve others which you may ask for specially. Check the list at the back of this book.

By the time your child is a year old you will hopefully have met your local educational psychologist and, if there is one in your area, the pre-school advisory teacher for children with special educational needs. If you have not met them, and would like their help and advice, contact them through your local Education Office. They can visit you at home, assess your child's development and offer helpful advice on different toys, games and activities which you can use with your child to help his progress and prepare him for school. Often a Portage worker is available (either a trained teacher or Community Nurse) who will assess the child's needs and recommend a programme to help the child's development. Portage is an early intervention programme prepared for young children with special educational needs, or who are slow learners, from birth to five years. It covers all areas of development in the very young child – language (and communication) skills, self-help skills, social skills, physical development and cognitive development. These will be discussed in the next chapter.

In the early months of your child's life support is available from your paediatrician, family doctor, health visitor and members of the medical and health professions. As well as making your own visits to the family doctor and baby clinic, you will probably find your paediatrician will wish to keep himself informed about your child's all-round development, health and general well-being. He will probably do this by organising regular case conferences to which parents and child will be invited as well as other professional people who are also concerned with different aspects of your child's development. These people are all members of the 'multi-disciplinary team' and will be actively concerned with your child's progress and with ensuring that his individual needs are being met.

This is a chance for everyone involved to make sure that everything that is possible is being done to help the child and the family, particularly as he grows older. Is his body growing satisfactorily? Is he keeping healthy? Can he see and hear as well as he should be able to? If not, is there anything that can be done to improve things? How well can he do things for himself? Can he speak clearly or would he benefit from a speech therapist (who can help with language development as well as difficulties in articulation or pronunciation)? Any family or financial difficulties can be referred to the social worker for advice. You probably had one appointed in the early days via the hospital to offer help and discuss the implications of your child's condition. He or she will also be able to discuss and explain any benefits which you are entitled to.

As the child approaches school age the psychologist's advice may be sought and local provision for the education of children with special needs and learning difficulties discussed. A suitable placement can then be made to cater for the child's particular individual needs. Before starting school, however, it may be decided that the child would benefit from an earlier placement at a playgroup, nursery class or short-term placement at a diagnostic and assessment unit. Annual conferences of this kind are held to see that any changes in the child's needs are being met in the best possible way.

Special Education makes provision for all children with learning difficulties, who cannot achieve properly within the mainstream school. This includes both mental and physical disabilities and various other problems resulting in learning difficulties. Children with special needs may often be slow in developing in more than one area; the special educational curriculum looks at all aspects of growth and development in relation to the individual child and his needs. It is concerned with the child as an individual and his total development and well-being. In some instances, particularly for deaf or blind children, education may be available from an age as early as two years.

The educational psychologist and pre-school advisory teacher form part of this service. When assessing your child's development, and suggesting things for you to do, they may refer to early development guidelines such as Portage, noting things he is able to do and describing more activities for you to try with your child. Children with Down's Syndrome invariably experience delay in the acquisition of spoken language skills. Parents, teachers and carers may find that a signing vocabulary, such as Makaton, can be used effectively to accompany speech, enhance the child's ability to understand and communicate and relieve frustration when the child is unable to make his needs known. This can be discussed with the speech therapist and will be referred to again in Chapter 2.

The stimulation which a child receives from an early age lays the essential foundation on which to build future progress and achievement. Indeed, a child starts to learn from the very moment he is born and continues to do so throughout his life. Education has been described as happening from the cradle to the grave. These early years are especially vital, as are the wealth of experiences which accompany them – and how much more so for a child starting out with a disability!

Social experience
Young children need to meet and play with other children and adults. In this way they learn to accept other people around them, starting with their own family circle and extending outwards to include friends and relatives. They will then be ready to play alongside, and then *with* one or two other children, before becoming part of a group of other young children. They are now ready to take another step towards the wider world. You will probably then be looking around for a suitable

playgroup or nursery school for your child to attend. Children learn so much just from being with other children, sharing activities, and being encouraged to join in and do the same as others. In the words of an old Chinese proverb, 'I hear, and I forget. I see, and I remember. I do, and I *understand.*'

Checklist: Steps in development

1. Infant stimulation

Visual Ideas and things to use:
   Bright objects   _____
   Mobiles   _____
   Pictures   _____
   Toys – string across cot or pram _____
   Moving objects   _____
   Prop him up to see familiar people
    and surroundings   _____

Auditory Make use of:
   Toys and objects with different
    sounds   _____
   Talking and singing   _____

Touch Give experience of toys and objects which are:
   Soft   _____
   Furry or fluffy   _____
   Smooth   _____
   Rough   _____

Communication Healthy signs of development:
   Sucks   _____
   Smiles   _____
   Cries   _____
   Coos   _____
   Stops crying when need is met _____
   Follows object or sound with eyes _____

Physical Encourage him to:
   Push with arms and legs   _____

Turn head _____

Roll over _____

Reach for objects _____

Grasp objects _____

---

2. Early development

Social Encourage him to:

Smile _____

Vocalise _____

Accept toys _____

Touch and pat familiar
people and toys _____

Respond to adult and toys _____

Play with toys _____

Play Encourage him to:

Hold and release _____

Place objects in and on _____

Put pieces together and take them
apart _____

Build with bricks _____

Stack cups _____

Language Signs of healthy development:

Vocalises _____

Makes and copies different sounds _____

Recognises and responds to
well-known people and objects _____

Uses animal sounds _____

Recognises nursery rhymes and
action songs _____

Listens to you talking _____

Shares books and games while you
talk about them _____

Talks about what you see and do
on trips _____

Speech Signs of healthy development:

Names familiar persons and objects _____

Uses meaningful words (keep a
   record)   _____
Uses new words regularly   _____
With a bigger vocabulary uses two
   words together   _____
Licks lollies   _____
Sucks through straws   _____
Blows bubbles   _____
Plus: brush his teeth and tip of
   tongue   _____

'Signing' as a means of communication:

Can precede or accompany normal
   speech   _____
Discuss with speech therapist or
   pre-school advisory teacher   _____

Self-help Positive signs:

Drinks from a cup   _____
Feeds with a spoon   _____
Holds out arm or leg to be dressed_____
Sits on pot or toilet   _____
Takes off clothes   _____
Washes face and hands   _____
Puts foot in shoe   _____

Cognitive Can match:

Texture   _____
Colour   _____
Shape   _____
Size   _____
Objects to picture   _____

Objects to fit in place   _____
Body parts   _____

Physical Signs of healthy development:

Moves to reach things   _____
Kicks, stretches, rolls, turns   _____
Sits, crawls, stands, walks   _____
Pushes and pulls toys   _____
Rolls a ball   _____

Marks paper with crayon   _____
Picks up and places objects   _____
Builds with bricks   _____

---

3. Sources of help

Check your contacts:

Doctor   _____
Paediatrician   _____
Social worker   _____
Health visitor   _____
Baby clinic   _____
Community nurse   _____
Support groups   _____
Down's Syndrome Association   _____
Mencap   _____
Parent-Toddler group   _____
Library   _____
Speech therapist   _____
Pre-school advisory teacher   _____
Educational psychologist   _____
Portage worker   _____

2
Tears and Smiles: The Toddler Stage

Individual personality

By now you will see a pattern of development emerging. Children rarely progress along a regular upward trend. Their own feelings and personality will interact. They will display normal feelings (not always socially acceptable!) of pleasure, anger and frustration, and the inevitable temper tantrums normal among all two-year-olds. Try to take all these in your stride and recognise the fact that your toddler *is* an individual and does need to express his own feelings – feelings after all that are natural to all of us at almost any age. You can always try to divert his attention to a more useful or rewarding task. Don't pay *too* much attention, either, to bad behaviour of which you don't approve; you will only reinforce it. Children are experts at seeking attention and they will soon learn that bad behaviour is a quick and easy way to get it! Instead, see that he gets plenty of praise and attention for *good* behaviour. He will then soon learn in a rewarding way what is more socially acceptable – not only to you but to other people too. 'Why is it that all his bad habits are so-called normal behaviour?' I was once asked by a distraught mother as her young child employed yet another delaying tactic at bedtime!

All children have their ups and downs in everyday life, and as they grow and learn they are bound to have their good days and their bad days, just like adults. We have all had days when everything seems to go along fine and we're riding high on the crest of a wave, and there are other days that often start off wrong and then nothing seems to go right for us. Usually children with Down's Syndrome are blessed with a happy, sunny nature. Many make friends easily and go readily to other people. Their trusting and accepting nature as well as their joy and pleasure is expressed in a very open way.

There are times, of course, when an obstinate streak shows through.

34

But, be honest, which of *us* has never been obstinate? Once they dig their toes in it can be like trying to move a mountain! One of my pupils refused to read to me and I suddenly realised that I had not heard him read for a week and could find no way of teasing or persuading him into doing so. I felt very guilty. How could I, his teacher, keep a check on his progress if he was only reading at home and not at school? (Yes! children with Down's Syndrome can and do read.) In this case I tried that old-fashioned tactic, bribery. I rewarded him with a sweet when he came and read to me in the quiet room (away from distractions). Luckily it worked and he soon came to read readily enough; two weeks later he did not even look for the sweet afterwards.

But the same ploy failed with another child who adamantly shut his mouth. The whole expression on his face clearly stated that in no way was he going to read. Persuasion and bribery did not solve the problem. He dug his toes in and refused to budge! He has been known to do this in other situations, too, and his parents have often said that he will 'cut off his nose to spite his face'!

Not to be out-manoeuvred by this young man, I handed out reading books and word cards as usual. I was showing that this was the time when we all had a reading session, and put his book in front of him. I was not going to force him to read (in fact I couldn't) – just making the point that it was 'reading time'. My helper and I were both busy with two of the other children when I glanced across at the young lad in question. Not only had he opened his book and found the page, but he was pointing to the words and mouthing them. Although he uttered not a sound I just knew, and could tell, that he was silently absorbed in the story. How's that for a silent reading lesson? He also proved that he could and would do it – but *in his own time*. He also conformed to the classroom situation in his own way, having asserted his individual personality.

Even in a small group of similar children, within the same age group and within a limited range of ability, you will find that each one has their own characteristics and personality traits. They have their own family, background and inherited features. They experience their own environment and will respond to the stimulus which they receive from it, and will grow up in their own unique way.

Personal development

Let's take a look at the individual child. Personal growth and development, I believe, can only be measured on an individual basis – which is why I never wish to compare the progress of children in my care to that of others. Each child is an individual and as far as possible should be assessed as such, and his progress related to his *own* merits. Having said this I know that parents will he heartened to hear that other children are at a similar stage. You can gain a lot of comfort, and feel less anxious when you find that similar children are capable of similar skills. We will look at the individual development of the whole child within five broad areas: communication, self-help, social, physical, and cognitive development.

Children communicating

The ability to understand and to communicate are of paramount importance in human experience. Learning starts from the very beginning of life. A small baby has needs and feelings which require a response. If he is hungry he cries; he will show pleasure when fed. He soon gets to recognise the face that will feed him and will stop crying when he is picked up. Why? – because he understands that his need will be attended to. First steps in learning! He will look around and become familiar with faces and everyday objects. He will get to know well-known sounds and communicate his feelings by expressing his own noises of pleasure, demand and distress.

Communication then has its origins right at the start of life, but this is a two-way process and does require a response. Even if your child has difficulty in making sounds or being able to talk, if he is slow or unwilling to talk, don't despair. Never give up talking to him for you will deprive him of hearing the spoken word. *Hearing* speech and language is essential to his understanding of it, and provides a good example for him to follow. Encourage him to express his own feelings and needs and involve him in conversation with others. Try not to speak *for* him, or talk *about* him in his presence as if he wasn't there; give him every opportunity to communicate for himself. How often have I asked a child a question only to get an answer from the adult with him, when I knew that the child was quite capable of speaking for himself!

Involve him, even if you have to provide the answer at first. At tea time daddy might arrive home and say, 'Hello. What did you do today?' Silence. 'Tell daddy you went to the park.' The response may be another silence, but even if it just produced 'yes' you will have achieved something, especially if his eyes light up with pleasure and his face beams as he remembers the pleasure of the trip. One important event will often stand out in a child's mind from a day crowded with exciting incidents. I remember one such eventful day including a ride in a car to the railway station (we had to stop on the way in a cloud of steam because the radiator of the car boiled dry) and a ride in a train up the beautiful river valley and over a bridge, watching boats and cows on the way followed by a walk in the sun; but the experience that captivated one particular child was a visit we paid to a friend's house.

On another occasion we had been thoroughly entertained at the local police station. The children handled a police dog and watched him retrieve certain articles; they were let loose in the traffic control cars (much to the annoyance of the neighbours I am sure), had their fingerprints taken and were shown the cell – where they all had to try out the toilet! Back at school, the normal routine of the day took over. Happily, message books accompany the children between home and school. Not one of the children arrived home bursting to tell of their exciting morning spent at the police station until they were asked, 'What did you do today?' No response. Prompt: 'Did you go to the police station?' 'Oh yes . . . !' Then the floodgates opened and they were all bursting to relate their experiences.

Communication is just like a telephone: messages can be given and received in both directions. Your child needs to listen and understand, and then communicate. Understanding is based on his knowledge of previous experiences; he then has to express himself, through noises at first, crying and gurgles, and cooing noises in imitation of adult talk. Learning to speak means copying those around him. Make sure that he has plenty to listen to. Babbling and experimenting with sound will lead to his first words which are often 'daddy' and 'mummy' which is very rewarding for you! More words will be learned by naming things after you. This develops into shortened sentences (telegraphic speech) such as 'daddy car' or 'mummy tea'. Singing nursery rhymes and songs will encourage listening to full length sentences, and help the child to pick up the rhythm and intonation. If they feel pleasurable and enjoyable he will try them out for himself. Again, let him try to express his own feelings and needs, recount a recent event, talk about a television programme and name pictures in a book. These will all help his progress. Expressing thoughts is more difficult and comes later on as a result of reinforcing and building further upon these early utterances, and of course with more experience of life. Writing, too, comes at a later stage, as does reading.

Children with Down's Syndrome nearly always experience delay in speech acquisition. This can be frustrating for parents, teachers and carers, not to mention the child himself! Indeed, some children may have problems with articulation and a long-term difficulty producing speech that can be clearly understood. In this instance the speech therapist may recommend the introduction of a signing vocabulary such as Makaton. Makaton has been successfully introduced to facilitate and enable communication. The adults – parents, teachers and carers – use a basic sign language to accompany speech and encourage the child to sign too. This continues as the child attempts and develops speech. This can be used as a transition stage until the child develops his own speech, and the signing can then fade. If the child continues to experience difficulty with the spoken word then the use of Makaton (or signing) may continue for as long as it is felt necessary. The child is then able to communicate with others and to make himself understood. Makaton was devised to overcome the difficulty in communication experienced by children and young people with learning difficulties and language delay.

More recently, research has been carried out and progress made in developing language and reading skills among young children with Down's Syndrome by the Portsmouth Project. Here reading has been used to develop language skills. The Project has also involved the family in working with the child under the direction of a 'home tutor'. The child is taught to match and name familiar persons and objects in his everyday life, first with pictures and then with cards. The words are used regularly every day and the vocabulary of both speaking and reading are increased and developed following the pattern of normal language development. Further information can be obtained from the Portsmouth Project and Down's Syndrome Association. Can he see and hear similar and dissimilar things? Can he match similar shapes and objects? Can he complete a simple jigsaw, form board and pattern sequence? Does he enjoy looking at picture books, talking about them and pointing to things in the picture? Does he enjoy listening to stories and joining in songs and rhymes? I mentioned earlier the importance of talking to your child. But explain things to him, too.

Pre-reading and pre-number skills are very similar. Many of the activities involve playing with toys and objects, especially matching shapes and colours, and putting things into and onto pegs or boxes. Provide plenty of toys to play with at home and chat to your child while you're doing it. The importance of language cannot be stressed enough, so talk and explain freely. Language is an organic growth activity that can be used in each and every situation. You will also find how pleased he will be when you praise and encourage him. It will give him so much confidence to try again. Do show him how to do things; children – all children – love copying. By imitating others he will learn so much. By copying skills that you will be showing him he will start to learn to look after himself.

Helping your child to help himself is very important to him; it will aid his confidence and self-esteem, and encourage him to be more independent and responsible for himself. Even if at times it is a long and tedious job, it is well worth it in the long run. For if you never give him the chance to dress himself, put on his shoes, pick up his bag, open the door, get in the car and so on, when will he ever learn? And I am sure that you as a parent certainly do not wish to be doing things like this as he grows bigger and older, into his teens or even into adulthood!

Self-help skills

Naturally all parents have the same problem at this stage, as there is not always enough time to wait and watch. Start a task earlier, if possible, and give him enough time to do the task for himself. As I said, it is far better in the end for the child to say 'do it myself', as one of my own young charges now adamantly insists. She is five years old and it is a joy to watch her grow daily in confidence and independence.

Many special schools – those providing for children with more severe learning difficulties – teach 'self-help' skills as part of the school curriculum. The aim is to help each individual child, as far as possible, to become an independent and responsible member of the community. Just pause for a moment and take a look around you at other adults and children and ask yourself these questions. What is it that we all have to learn to do to grow up? What are the first things that we have to learn in order to become independent? If you discover an answer that is the same for all of us it will most likely be 'to look after ourselves'. This is something which we all have to do, at whatever level we function.

Treat your child as a normal human being and let him do things for himself. If he never tries he will never learn. It may mean a mess and it might take time and patience. Show him how to take his pants down, sit on the toilet, and pull his pants up again, then how to wash his hands afterwards. Show him in small steps: roll up sleeves, put in plug, turn tap, pick up soap, rub hands, rinse hands, pull out the plug and dry his hands. Try *backward chaining*: let the child try the last move (i.e. the last link in the 'chain') by himself first. When he can do that, let him try the one before, and work backwards until he can perform the whole sequence by himself. Try to adopt the same methods for other complicated tasks. You will be surprised to find how many small steps are involved in doing something which as adults we take for granted. How many small separate moves are involved in tying up a shoelace, for instance? Break it down and count each move. Can you find eleven or more?

Teach him how to brush his teeth and comb his hair, to blow his nose. Let him try to put on his own clothes and undress himself. Not all at once! Try the easy stages first, with easy-to-manage clothes with no fastenings. Taking them off is easier than putting them on; we can get in a tangle here! For example, it is fairly easy to pull down trousers and to step out of them, whereas both feet frequently go into the same leg, and usually through the hem rather than the waist when first trying to put them on! Feeding oneself can be a very messy business too – but all toddlers go through this stage. Also, he may have fads and fancies regarding food. But ask yourself this: would *you* eat anything and everything that was put in front of you? It is very hard to make someone do something they just don't want to do, and it would be a shame for meal-times to degenerate into a battlefield.

One of my 'parents' was horrified when I explained that many special schools had teaching programmes for children to learn to use the toilet, wash their hands, feed themselves, dress and undress themselves. 'But that's the parents' job to teach them at home, not the school's,' she said. It has certainly made my job much easier! Since they are all reasonably proficient at these tasks, we can press ahead with more social and academic activities in school.

Social skills
Social competences, like self-help skills, are frequently learned by children within the family situation, too. Generally, one assumes that social manners and conduct are picked up from those around us – copied and learned from within the family circle or classroom at school. Many of these accomplishments, however, we find have to be outlined and systematically taught to our children, just as we show them how to brush their teeth or comb their hair.

In order to become socially acceptable we all have to conform to certain standards of behaviour, a general code of conduct accepted by all. This form of behaviour, 'personal competence', may also appear very like the ability to look after oneself within the community. This would include such things as crossing the road safely, going on an errand and taking a message, and being able to find out where and how to catch a bus. We do not expect at the toddler stage for *any* child to be capable of doing these things for themselves. The experience gained will enable them to become familiar with and aware of these situations. In providing the opportunity we can be aiming in this direction.

The home influence will provide models to copy. The child will take its first steps into the outside world as a member of the family and later on as a member of a school. Social integration means getting along

Katie, aged four, riding at the donkey park.

happily with other people. It's a progression from the family circle, where children can interact with relatives and friends, on to playgroup or nursery school where they will be mixing with more children of their own age, whom they will get to know and be known by. This is almost the first step in becoming a member of the community. Other steps taken to increase the circle of acquaintances can be achieved by letting your child go with you on local trips to the park, shops and library, or to neighbourhood events such as summer fairs, autumn bazaars and the cinema and pantomine, as well as family trips and treats to theme parks and leisure centres.

Getting on with other people is very important. In the early stages he will start by playing with his toys by himself. The next stage is to play happily alongside other children. Then to be able to play with one other child, and gradually get used to joining in with a group of children before moving on to become part of a class at school. Being part of a group means learning how to share, how to wait and take one's turn, how to be polite and considerate towards others. This includes saying 'please' and 'thank you', 'good morning' and 'how are you?'. The five-year-old children that I work with have impressed my colleagues by these simple courtesies, not just at school but at birthday parties and in the local shops. They can ask politely for what they want and share toys quite happily. I also find that being able to play games with other children also helps them to be accepted. The children I teach can play snap, dominoes, ludo, snakes and ladders and other attractive but simple dice games better than many of the other infants who come and join us. Perhaps they have had more practice since we play games together as part of their early number work: I deliberately teach numbers one to six to start with, both counting and recognising the numerals. Dice are obtainable with either dots or numbers on them. All these games can be enjoyed within the family.

At a later stage you will want your child to be able to find his way around the community. By then he will have accompanied you on all kinds of family excursions. Try to find something different and exciting to do – visiting a zoo, adventure park, model railway or taking a ride on a train, bus or boat. Perhaps you could visit an aerodrome? These can all be very exciting with the fun shared by all the family. This is especially so when most car owners just drive from door to door these days. When did you last go on a bus or train? Simple experiences such as these can widen your child's interest and awareness of the world around.

By joining in community activities your child will not only get to know other people but will become accepted by them. Even more important, people will get to know him as an individual and you will find that he will be known for *who* he is and not what he is. Furthermore, as he learns to mix with other children, and copy them, you should find that he starts behaving just like others. He will naturally become part of the group and not stand out as being any different.

It is surprising how many people, probably with no previous experience of the condition, will display prejudice or even fear when first confronted by a child with special needs. Most admit that once they get to know the child as an individual they will respond to the personality; the 'label' as such will fade into insignificance and become immaterial.

Physical development
Playing with other children and being able to move around independently will call for a certain amount of mobility. At the toddler stage this is often at a very similar level to that of any toddler (once he has found his feet!). He may be slower to start to sit up, crawl or walk, but he will soon be toddling around like the other children. All children vary in their rate of progress and often will only do things when they feel instinctively ready to do so. Never give up! Keep providing that stimulation and encouragement. Play with him, talk to him and praise his efforts, not just his achievements. Help him develop awareness of his surroundings; give him things to interest him and place them so that he will have to move to get them, by rolling over, crawling or standing.

If he is not walking it may well be because other people just give him things he needs, so that he has no need to make an effort. Maybe he is crawling 'too well'! He can get there more quicly and can manage without getting up onto his feet, a laborious struggle. Are his muscles strong enough to take his weight? Is he exercising his legs? To strengthen them, make standing up fun by placing a favourite toy on a chair for him to stand against. Hold his hands while he plays football.

His development will follow the same pattern as for so-called 'normal' development, but he may need smaller steps along the way and more time and attention. But what is a 'normal' child anyway? We, all progress through life at our own pace, some faster, some slower than others, but each in our own time! Your child, with a bit more help and assistance, will get there in the end. You yourself will note each little step forward along the path of achievement. Each of these little steps is, in fact, another 'milestone' passed, and you can feel justifiably proud. He will walk when he is good and ready. In fact, when he does you will sometimes wish that he couldn't, for now, even more than at the crawling stage, he will be into everything he can reach!

To develop co-ordination and mobility of limbs give him big toys to play with so that he can rock, ride, push and pedal. Give him opportunities to climb (watch and guard the stairs at first!). Play ball with him, rolling, throwing, catching and batting. Let him play, dig in the sand, paddle (most children love water) and build with bricks. Dancing games can include running, jumping and skipping. Skipping may appear awkward at first as it involves more complex co-ordination, but a *lot* of five-year-olds find this a challenge!

As your child gains confidence in moving around give him plenty of opportunity to use his fingers, too. Just think for a minute how many different things we can do with our own fingers whether at work, in daily life, or for leisure pursuits – even intricate and delicate work. Finger control involves fine manipulation and the co-ordination of hand and eye movements.

Handling objects from an early age will help the ability to touch, sense, grasp and control. The instinct to explore comes naturally to all babies. The inevitable test is to put everything in the mouth! This, of course, is a baby's first sensor. The child finds out about the immediate environment by giving it the 'mouth test'. Is it food? Will he like it or find it distasteful? Is it hard or soft?

While playing with toys he will learn to hold and let go. This is another favourite game. How many times can he persuade mum to retrieve the rattle from the floor? Give him toys to squeeze and press, push and pull. There are lots of ingenious toys in the shops to interest babies and toddlers; they can provide almost endless sensory experience and stimulate curious little fingers. Some may be rather expensive! If you find this to be the case put them on your Christmas list (friends and relatives are sometimes at a loss as to what to buy). Or you may be able to borrow some from the toy library if there is one in your area. Your health visitor or pre-school advisory teacher should know of their existence.

Let him pick up shapes and place them in or on apparatus. Try doing jigsaws, threading beads, building bricks, putting together simple construction toys, screwing and unscrewing the lid on a jar. Allow play with sand, water, paint, playdough and make things to eat with real pastry. At the same time talk about shape and colour, try matching objects and telling the difference. He can try to scribble or make marks with crayons, chalk, felt pens and pencils; and you can draw his attention to bold simple outline shapes, patterns or pictures. When he is aware of the line drawing on the page he can trace this outline and colour in the area. There are sets of templates available, a square board with press-out shapes of objects. These can be used first of all for colouring and tracing inside the template – particularly useful when there is limited control. Once this skill has been mastered you can try holding the pressed-out shape with one hand and let the child draw around the outside of the object, feeling the edge with the pencil.

Cognitive development

We all start learning and developing through our infant play experiences. Play enabled us all as children to come to terms with our environment. Providing these opportunities, the stimulation to encourage your child to do things for itself, relate to other people, increase its own body awareness and develop its own particular skills, all contribute towards his cognitive development, too. In order to learn about the world in which it lives and to take part in it, the child needs to experience and understand both at home and at school.

Children with learning difficulties are apt to have a short attention span and limited awareness. However, if your child enjoys a task, takes pleasure in being able to complete it and finds it rewarding too, you will find that it also improves its attention. Once you have captured this attention the child can become fully involved and able to concentrate. Without this ability he cannot learn. A child who is easily distracted is unable to pay attention and concentrate, and will find it harder to learn. It will be just as difficult for those around it. A sense of achievement will result in self-confidence and a feeling of self-worth, which can flood across into other areas and activities. Success breeds success.

In order to reinforce understanding, see how well the child can respond to a command or carry out an instruction, whether it is to place one brick on top of another, put the toy car into the garage or point to a named object in a picture or story book. Does he understand cause and effect? If he shakes a rattle does he know it will make a noise? Can he copy? If you build a tower of bricks, can he do the same? Can he match similar shapes and colours and find different sizes? Can he replace shapes or figures in a form board or do simple jigsaws? Can he match objects to sounds or pictures? Can he copy straight lines (vertical and horizontal), circles and crosses? Can he name his clothes and different parts of his body? Can he copy a pattern or sequence by placing shapes or bricks or threading beads? How many colours can he identify?

The growth of thinking and understanding will depend upon all these early experiences. New activities and instructions have to be received, seen and heard, and processed in the brain. They will be matched with past events and understood within their context. In carrying out a verbal command or following a new task he needs to understand what is required of him, interpret the instruction and then give the right response in words or actions. If he has a problem in receiving or expressing himself, you may be able to pinpoint other difficulties. Can he actually see and hear well enough to receive the instruction? Can he relate it to previous experiences and so understand what is required? Is there anything hindering his response? – can he see what he is doing, hear what he is saying? Has he got enough finger control to put the object in the right place? He will need plenty of practice to learn a new skill and even more to reinforce and retain the learned skill and learning pattern.

Through playing with your child you will get to know him, his likes and dislikes, his strengths and weaknesses. You will also find out whether he has any special difficulties. Try to provide a variety of activities: if one seems not to work after you have given it a fair try, find an alternative. If he seems to have some recurring difficulty, discuss it with your doctor, social worker, paediatrician or someone else you feel able to talk to. They should be able to arrange for you to seek further advice, or to have his eyes or hearing tested.

Play and stimulation during these early years are vital to the child's future development and well-being, and the foundation is laid for all future learning. All early play experiences provide the child with a wealth of knowledge, perhaps not apparent at the time, but which makes a valuable contribution towards his future progress and achievements. We are all learning, all the time.

To encourage your child to become an independent and responsible citizen and family member, treat him as such. Respect his wishes and feelings, too. You are the one who knows your child best, and you will know that first and foremost he is a child like any other. This is the key. Any difficulty is of secondary significance.

If we could penetrate the prejudice and fear which still surround Down's Syndrome and learning difficulties, we would find that other people encounter this barrier through their own ignorance or lack of experience. They see the label, not the child. Their priorities are back to front. Like the shopkeeper, once you get to know the child as an individual you no longer notice the 'condition'; it simply loses its importance. See your child as a whole person. View his progress and well-being in the context of his whole development, and you should have a healthy, happy and busy little person on your hands. Above all, enjoy playing with your child. It should be both pleasurable and rewarding. He has so much to learn and you may well find that you have much to learn with him.

A member of the family

A full family member? – but of course! A child with Down's Syndrome is born into a family and has the same rights as all the other children. This child is your son or daughter and deserves all the love and support you would give to any child of yours. I said to one parent that I thought they had given their child a terrific amount of early stimulation during the pre-school years. 'Oh, I don't think so,' came the reply 'no more than we would to any child of ours.'

He may not be your first child; if he is you may decide to have another, or perhaps it is your decision to have only one. Whichever the choice, it is yours alone. The number of children in a family is always a personal matter for the parents. Whether you have one, two, three or more children, your child with Down's Syndrome is an important integral member of the whole family in his own right, and you can take equal pleasure and delight in him.

Bringing up any child has its rewards and disappointments, tears and smiles. The path through life is never easy or smooth running for any of us. There are many ups and downs in all family life – good days, not-so-good days, and problems to be overcome. It is only natural to show concern over a child's health, well-being, behaviour or progress. Try to adopt a positive attitude. Not always easy, I know, but praise and encouragement will bring their rewards. An attentive, concerned, relaxed and happy atmosphere will provide warmth and security in which to bring up your child. He too can respond naturally and happily. A sense of humour will not only help you through the bad patches but help you to make the most of the good times, too. If you feed and nurture your house plants they will thrive and flourish. How much more rewarding to nourish a child and watch him blossom, too, even though, as I overheard one American teacher say, he may be 'a late bloomer'!

All children have basic needs of affection, food, warmth, clothing and mental stimulation. These can be well provided for within the security of the family circle as well as school. Security here really is the key word. All children need security. They all have feelings and need to love and be loved. Your child will thrive on this. He feels safe within a familiar routine and surroundings. This forms the basis for his happiness and well-being, both now and in the future. He can develop within this environment and yet feel safe to venture out knowing he always has your support.

Family life means sharing, learning to give and take and being able to do things together. These are the roots of a future life, too. Learning to work and play together depends in adulthood on how we relate to our workmates and colleagues and how we mix socially. I have known teenagers with Down's Syndrome go out to work, go shopping, join youth clubs and go to dances just like any other young adult. How most people get on in adult life usually depends on how well they can get along with other people and cope socially. Many job skills can be learned at work, and do not have to be learned beforehand at school (although this may help). Obviously this does not apply in all cases, but for many jobs such as in factories, shops, working in a home, gardening, the actual skills required can often be learned in the job situation. It is all very well getting a job, but in my experience when working with school-leavers in special education (for children with learning difficulties) I have found that their ability to keep a job depends largely on how they get on with the people they are working with, rather than the tasks of the job itself.

Enjoying family life together includes making decisions, going on holidays and making excursions. In this you will be caring for your children while they savour new experiences. You have a shared project which gives you things to talk about and do together. Let your child join in and play his role as fully as he can.

One of the most enjoyable parts of my work is visiting family homes. It's such a pleasure to see how happily the children respond to the routine of a secure family life. On one occasion one little boy of six was at home after a short stay in hospital. He had helped mummy to make some jam-tarts in the morning and I was immediately invited into the kitchen to admire them. I was then shown into the living-room and offered a cup of coffee. The little boy carefully carried in the plate of tarts and offered me one – they were not spilt onto my lap! A little later his mother had to go out so he was left to help daddy get tea ready. He knew where all five in the family sat, where to get the cutlery and where to put it. He was busily occupied chattering away, making comments and showing that he could be very thoughtful and helpful, behaving quite naturally. He was completely 'at home' in the family atmosphere. It was a delight to see him playing his part as an important and valued member of the family. Thanks to this early care and devotion to his needs he has become a real credit to his family. He now goes to college and works part-time in the local supermarket.

Playgroups and nursery schools
Activities outlined in personal development (and many more) are part of the normal routine to be found in most playgroups and nursery

schools. They too aim to encourage the child's all-round development. Why not find out what opportunities exist in *your* neighbourhood? You may well find that these groups are over-subscribed, with a waiting list for places. Find out whether they are prepared to take children with special needs. Establishments catering for very young children often ask that the children have been toilet-trained before they accept them. Your health visitor, social worker or educational psychologist may be able to help you get your child a place; they will know how important it is for your child to get social and pre-school experience and the chance to mix and be accepted by others from an early age. They may be able to obtain extra help in caring for your child in this placement.

In recent years the opening up of playgroups and nursery provision has become more of a national trend; it has become increasingly recognised how vital these early formative years are to a child's well-being and future development. The mother plays an important role here, too, for she is the one constant presence, knows the child best and is responsible for his welfare at all times. It is up to you to make enquiries as to what is available near you. Seize the opportunity, and take full advantage of the resources provided; you won't regret it!

Playgroups and nursery classes provide a chance for children to get used to playing in groups and working alongside each other in preparation for school. This social training and experience will help them to share, take their turn, and respect the needs of others. Play activities will foster skills which will help their personal development and prepare them for future work in language, pre-reading and pre-number tasks.

Your child should benefit greatly from being able to join in with children of his own age and get used to routines ready for more organised activities at school. The most important point, I feel, is that he will become a member of the community very early on. He is not being 'sent away' to a special school or kept hidden out of sight. He will be accepted as a person in his own right.

The children in my class started school at the same time as the other children in the main school. When other children want to play they ask for my children by name. There is no stigma or differentiation between them. They are known for *who* they are and not what they are.

Playgroup or nursery school can encourage your child's development and social acceptance. It can provide relief for you, too, from being constantly vigilant towards a child who may need constant care and supervision. It can be a hard and exacting task to care for a special needs child, particularly one who demands a lot of your time and attention.

49

Relief and support

Most families feel that any problems they may have in caring for their child is theirs and theirs alone to sort out, and that they have to manage somehow. But it can sometimes be very demanding and leave you feeling very drained, in need of a valuable hour or so to yourself. There are schemes available which provide help and support if you feel that the family and child would benefit from some relief. These may be able to offer part-time, day, weekend or in some instances a longer period of care if necessary.

The social worker is the best person to ask about this, since he or she will know what kind of provisions are available. If you do not have a social worker already do contact your local Social Services Department. The address and telephone number can be found in the local phone book. Some families have one to visit fairly soon after the birth of a baby with Down's Syndrome.

You may not wish anyone else to look after your baby (a very natural feeling), or you may feel guilty that you are admitting that you cannot cope alone. But there's no need for that! It's hard work caring for any young child, even more so if it has some disability. There may come a time too when you have to cope by yourself. This can happen when husbands are in the services, or their work takes them away. There may be other family commitments to attend to, an illness in the family – or you may become ill yourself. Perhaps other chilren in the family are being deprived of your attention as a result of the time devoted to a special needs member. One young lady told how her studying for GCSE exams was frequently interrupted because her mother needed help to feed or change her young multi-disabled brother. She didn't mind helping, but once her studying was interrupted it was hard to get back into it again.

If your child is difficult to handle, even a minor shopping expedition can turn into a major disaster, resulting in frayed tempers all round and half the necessary purchases forgotten or abandoned in the effort! 'I can't even go shopping with her,' one mother was heard to say about her child. 'It's most embarrassing. She won't stop screaming and shouting, and she keeps pulling things off the shelves.' I had a similar report from a mother with a bright, lively normal two-year-old! Up pops the age-old question – what *is* normal behaviour?

You may feel awkward too at asking a friend, however willing, to babysit to give you an hour in peace. It is not an admission of defeat or failure to ask for help. We all need help at some time or another. If the services are available, there will be people trained and ready to help. Seek their support – you will gain a much needed break and return refreshed. Your child, too, may well benefit from a break and a chance to make friends in a new environment. You may well make new friends yourself! There could be several benefits all round.

Schemes in operation differ up and down the country depending on resources available and financial budgets. They vary from hostel provisions to care within a family and may be referred to as hostels, units, relief, link or family support schemes. All provide trained people ready to care for children with special needs. They will probably have organised play and activities to meet the children's needs and night time care, all under supervision. Link and family support schemes try to link families together, providing relief for those needing it.

It is becoming widely recognised today that families with a special needs member are 'special needs families'. The needs of the family *as a whole* need to be taken into account, not just those of the special needs member. With link and family support schemes the child is accepted into the support family home and cared for as part of the family, getting to know another 'aunty' and 'uncle' and other children as friends. These families usually get paid for their services; however, this is often organised through the Social Services and you yourself may not be asked to contribute. The amount of time which a child spends being looked after depends greatly upon his, or your, needs at the time. It may be as little as an hour or two now and again, perhaps a weekend, or even longer if the need arises and arrangements can be made.

If you feel that you would like to use this provision, please don't wait until you are desperate. Otherwise you may find that your child is suddenly thrust upon strangers who, though concerned to help, have not previously met him. Nor will the child feel secure or happy if pushed at a moment's notice into unfamiliar and bewildering surroundings. You, the other adults involved, and the child himself will be much happier if you have all made contact and got to know each other beforehand. The child, too, will be more ready to accept the situation if he is already familiar with the place and has been able to make friends with the people there. You will feel more relaxed knowing that he is being looked after properly and that you have had a chance to discuss some of his habits, routines, likes and dislikes. It is worth taking the time to introduce your child and ease him gently into this new set-up.

You may also find, particularly if your child is anxious about meeting new people, that the situation will be eased by inviting the support family or parents into your own home first. This way they can get to know him in his own surroundings and you can have a cup of tea, play and talk together, before introducing him to their home. Again, you may wish to go along with your child on his first visit to his new friend's house and let him know that everything is all right. He will be much happier then to go another time without you, when you are in need of relief. Similarly, if you are using the hostels or units you might find it a good idea, to start with, to take him there on a visit yourself.

Even if you feel that you don't need this help now, you may find that you can benefit from it later on as your child grows older. Parents often find that caring for a child with special needs may deprive the other children in the family of their time and attention.

Children with Down's Syndrome do not necessarily have a severe learning difficulty or exhibit challenging behaviour. In many cases it may not even be immediately apparent. Then you may feel that you and your family are able to manage the ups and downs of normal everyday family life just like anyone else. Many parents I have spoken to assure me that they can get along very well and that their child is not difficult to look after, and that it does not hinder any family activity. Other parents have admitted that life can be tough-going (especially if they are getting sleepless nights or have a young baby to manage, too). All have been glad of a chance to use the services provided, and all have benefited personally from the experience.

I know of one family giving support who have so taken to their new charge that they even asked if they can have him to share a special family outing, and have included him in their own family photographs proudly displayed in the front room!

There could be facilities near by – but you may find that you need to make enquiries since these services may not be very well advertised or known.

Financial assistance
Seeking family relief and support is a personal decision for you, even though you may receive advice and encouragement. However, there are financial benefits to which you are entitled if you have a special needs child, in the same way that you will be eligible for Child Benefit. In other words, these benefits are yours by right. The various benefits and allowances will depend on your circumstances and the needs of your child. Leaflets and information on all types of benefit can be obtained from any Social Security Office or Benefits Office.

If you have a child with Down's Syndrome you will usually qualify for a Disability Living Allowance. If there are problems with caring for the child at night, a night time allowance may also be available. This allowance is yours by right and does not depend on a means test.

To obtain this you will need to fill in a form from the Department of Social Security for a Disability Living Allowance (DLA). You will be eligible for the care component if the child needs a lot of care and attention (i.e. more than another child of the same age). The DLA includes a higher rate to include night care (when needed) and a mobility component if the child is five years or over and needs help with getting around – either they experience difficulties themselves or they need someone with them to help them to find their way around. In severe cases there may be eligibility for the Invalid Care and Severe Disability Allowance. If the parent(s) is/are in receipt of Income Support, a Disability Premium may be added to these payments.

Caring for a baby or toddler with special needs is very much like caring for any other baby. However, by the time a normal child reaches the age of about two years he is usually reasonably able and independent, whereas a special needs child still demands a great deal of the parents' time in terms of general care. He may not yet be toilet-trained or able to feed himself satisfactorily; perhaps he falls over or is still crawling. He may be wet, or soil at night. All this means frequent changes of clothing and a great mound of washing. If he is unable to do much for himself a great deal of his parents' time is taken up caring for him; he will need their constant attention and time, sometimes throughout the night if he is restless or disturbed during his sleep.

If you have any difficulties with the forms or applications to obtain your benefits, or indeed any other problems about your child or family needs, do contact the Social Security Office. There is also a Freephone telephone line available to help people with specific enquiries. Social workers are also there to help you. They have the contacts, expertise and knowledge of the law, and will be able to help with many problems and advise you on your rights. If you don't ask them, they may well think that you are managing all right and do not need any assistance! So never be afraid to ask. There may be other resources you could use. Go and find out. You may find, too, that local parent groups have even more specific information than health visitors or social workers whose work by its very nature is more general. This brings to mind another point which few parents seem to be aware of: you may also be entitled to disposable nappies or incontinence pads if your child still needs them. This service is usually available through the local NHS Trust; your health visitor should be able to advise you here. But if you have any difficulty, just ask your social worker for advice.

On other occasions, when you need help with some particular problem, you will probably go and see your family doctor or health visitor. As when consulting a social worker, they should be able to link you in to other specialist services. For instance, if your child continues to be incontinent you may find that a trained Community Nurse in Learning Disabilities can advise and discuss what products, treatment or medication could help.

Similarly you may be having difficulty with the child's behaviour, aspects of which may be unacceptable, distressing, or just irritating. In this case, a visit from the clinical psychologist may well throw a new light on the problem. He may be able to offer constructive advice on how to improve or correct such behaviour.

Families with severely disabled children may also qualify for financial assistance from various charitable organisations either nationally or locally. They can be of particular help when an expensive item is needed which will be of benefit to the child. Some other benefits available to help financially will include Child Benefit, free dental treatment, vouchers towards the cost of glasses and eye tests. Any others will depend on personal needs and circumstances.

All in all, in bringing up a child with special needs you need not feel isolated. There is plenty of help and support, and people concerned to care, understand and offer positive help. If help and resources are available, and you have a right to them, then do take full advantage of them for the well-being and benefit of you, your child, and the family as a whole.

Checklist: The toddler stage

1. Encourage early skills

Join in with   Family   _____
                      Friends   _____
                      Playgroup   _____

Get to know   Local community   _____
                      Shops   _____
                      Park   _____
                      Library   _____

Get used to other children(stages)
                      Play on own   _____
                      Play alongside another child   _____
                      Play with a small group   _____

Get used to	Sharing	_____
	Taking turns	_____
	Being polite	_____
	Considering other people	_____

---

2. Communication. Encourage him to:

Listen   to other people   _____

Understand   other people   _____

Use vocal expression

	Recognise people	_____
	Recognise names	_____
	Recognise objects	_____
	Recognise body parts	_____
	Recognise clothes	_____

Respond by saying

	Yes	_____
	No	_____
	Please	_____
	Thank you	_____
	Hello	_____
	Goodbye	_____

Note: Keep a list of words he knows and use them
   daily   _____
Carry out instructions   _____

---

3. Encourage self-help skills

	Use toilet	_____
	Wash	_____
	Eat and drink	_____
	Brush teeth	_____
	Comb hair	_____
	Take off clothes (with help)	_____
	Put on clothes (with help)	_____
	Put coat on peg	_____

Put clothes on chair _____

Open and close boxes, doors, etc. _____

Sit on chair _____

Sit on big toys _____

Get in and out of car _____

---

4. Encourage cognitive skills

Help understanding and awareness through play and games:

Matching _____

Playing with patterns _____

Puzzles _____

Using form boards _____

Using pegs _____

Playing with boxes _____

Playing with dolls house _____

Using toy cars and garage _____

Playing with farm and
zoo animals _____

Look at and talk about picture
books _____

Play games like snap _____

Dominoes _____

Throwing dice/dice games _____

---

5. Encourage motor skills

Body control   Sitting up _____

Rolling _____

Crawling _____

Standing up _____

Walking _____

Running _____

Jumping _____

Dancing _____

Climbing _____

Playing with ball (roll, throw, kick,
catch, hit) _____

Play with big toys (ride, rock,
push) _____

Finger control   Experience different textures   _____
Play with sand   _____
Play with water   _____
Use paint   _____
Use playdough   _____
Play with pastry   _____
Mark and draw with crayon or
   chalk   _____
Touch, grasp, hold, let go   _____
Squeeze, press, shake, push, pull   _____
Build with bricks   _____
Place beads on pegs   _____
Thread beads, unscrew jar cap   _____
Press buttons   _____
Trace (inside, on top, outside)   _____
Colour inside shapes/outlines   _____
Draw circle and straight line   _____

Note: notice how long he concentrates on a task and notice improvements.

---

6. Resources for you and your child

Check   Parent groups   _____
Toy library   _____
Playgroup   _____
Assessment unit   _____
Makaton sign language   _____
Family link schemes   _____
Relief care   _____

Information on
Child Benefit   _____
Income Support   _____
Disability Living Allowance   _____
Charities   _____
Disposable nappies   _____
Learning development aids   _____
Early learning   _____

3
Exploding the Myth: Starting School

Feelings and emotions

Starting school is a big step in any child's life. Suddenly, they are babies no longer. As the child is dressed in a smart new school uniform and bundled off to school, perhaps in a school bus or taxi, parents are left at home feeling very strange and different. They may have most of the day to themselves with an unfamiliar empty feeling, wondering what to do now that they do not have to concern themselves constantly with the demands of their youngster.

The child too will feel strange at first as he walks into school to be greeted by his new teacher, a whole new routine ahead of him. If he is quite happy and is looking forward to these new experiences parents will have no need to worry about him. If they feel happy and relaxed about it they will be helping *him* to accept the new environment and thus feel more secure in himself, since he will take his cue from his parents. Children respond very quickly to feelings of anxiety or pleasure from those around them, particularly those close to them such as their parents, teachers and carers.

The right preparation and a positive introduction will help the child to respond and accept the new situation. If he has been fortunate he will already have experienced mixing with other children and adults by attending a playgroup or nursery school. He will thus be ready to go on to full-time education, and should have no problem at all in fitting in. Children who miss out on these early years of social integration and education experiences, who perhaps have never been separated from mummy before, may well find this new situation stressful and bewildering. They will take much longer to settle in and get used both to the new adults caring for them and to the building in which they will spend the greater part of each day.

If the child is used to different adults looking after him such as friends, neighbours and playgroup helpers, he will more readily accept the authority of his new teacher and the many staff involved in special education. He will get to know many other adults, starting with classroom helpers, escorts and bus or taxi drivers. Soon after he will get to know the headteacher, school secretary, dinner-time helpers and school cooks. He will probably also meet the school doctor, school nurse, educational psychologist, speech therapist, peripatetic teacher to test hearing, dentist, students and visitors to the school. If he is used to meeting other people and playing with them he should be able to respond well, whether by answering 'good morning' politely, consenting to a medical examination, helping with an assessment, or chatting to a visitor.

Preparing for school
As well as meeting many adults the child will join in many activities with other children, not just in the same class, but with other children in the same school. Children like playing with other children; it comes naturally, and is part of their normal development. They should be encouraged to play with friends and visit relations, too. If they have already been to playgroup they will have become used to playing alongside and with other children. They will know how to join in and take their turn with others; they will learn to consider other people as well as themselves. Special needs children do not need to stand out or be any different from other children. They need the chance to mix with others and be shown how to behave towards them. They can learn many skills quickly and retain this knowledge. You will often find that once learned it is never forgotten! – especially if there are plenty of chances to practise. If they are aware of situations and understand the circumstances, you will also find that they are able to understand cause and effect. Everyone responds to praise and reward, including your children – and even you! You may well be rewarded by now for your efforts in giving your time and attention to your child's needs, for they like 'helping' too. Children can be delightfully thoughtful and con-siderate. I have seen the pride and pleasure on parents' faces when they have watched their own child with Down's Syndrome, without any prompting, go and fetch a chair for a visitor, carry a parcel for a friend, or open a door for a lady with a pushchair – at six or seven years old!

Most children with Down's Syndrome, in my experience, display no inhibitions. Indeed, they have a natural zest for life, and show no animosity towards anyone. Their exuberance can carry them through the day; they have a gift for enjoying life to the full and making the most of every occasion. Let them enjoy life, it can be fun! – and so much more rewarding. Let's provide these opportunities and make the most of them, rather than repressing enthusiasm and imposing a dull and boring routine. Their natural friendliness, too, will enable them to be accepted by their peer group – children of their own age – especially in these early years; very young children have not yet learned fear and prejudice. Likewise there are no barriers to communication. I have often watched a group of young children playing together and chattering away. As a mere adult I had not understood a single word, but the children themselves were quite busy and happy! Another advantage of attending a local playgroup, if your child will be attending a local school, is that when he moves on to school he will already be known by the other children when they go to school together, and by other children in the neighbourhood.

Educational provision
Not all children, unfortunately, will be so lucky. Some may have to travel away to a school providing for their particular needs; there may not be one in your immediate area. This will depend to some extent on whether you live in an urban or rural community. I have known one little boy who only had to walk around the corner to get to school, and another little five-year old who had to travel twenty-five miles in a taxi each way!

These days a 'statement' may be made as to the child's needs, which parents will help to prepare. We will look at the making of this statement later in the chapter. Following the statement a recommendation will be made for an educational provision best suited to meet these needs. Again parents will be consulted and have a right to say what they feel. Provision will largely depend on what is available in the area, and this may vary considerably from one local authority to another. Parents may well have very strong feelings about what sort of education and school they want their child to have. Remember, parents do have a right to have a say. After all, it is their child's future which is being considered, and what is being planned is the next eleven years or so of his life.

How should we see the main aim of education? The answer, in general terms, used to be a 'preparation for life'. But, what *is* a preparation for life, and how can it be achieved? Educational aims are constantly under review today. What do you wish for your child? How can his particular needs be met? It was once commonly thought that children with Down's Syndrome couldn't learn – but they are increasingly showing us that they can and will – given the right opportunities. Once they used to be put away from view but today they

Tom, aged five, listening to story books with a friend.

are able to fulfil their own role and take their own place within the community. Who knows, with the right opportunities, experiences and attention to their needs, what they may be achieving in the years ahead?

Educational placement may be recommended within a special school. This might be a school for children with severe learning difficulties or one for those with moderate learning difficulties. In either case the children are being removed from the community to a special school with specially trained staff, resources, and a curriculum designed to cater for their individual needs, as well as an entitlement to the National Curriculum.

Alternatively, provision may be met within a special Unit. This is usually built onto, or as part of, a main school. In some cases the Unit may be quite independent of the main school and function on its own. In this case the child will receive specialist educational treatment, resources and curriculum within the Unit; at the same time he'll be 'going to school' alongside other children in the area, but not necessarily mixing with them educationally or socially.

The second type of Unit is one attached to the main school. Whilst providing specialist education it can also offer opportunities for integrating with normal school activities, and for mixing educationally and socially with the other children in the school. In some local authority areas you may find that there is an Area Special Class for some children with learning difficulties who cannot cope independently within a large mainstream class. (Special Schools and classes generally have fewer children in each class because the children need more individual attention than is possible in an ordinary school.) In some educational authorities you may find that children with special needs can be fully integrated into an ordinary class; this trend appears to be on the increase. Much depends on the behaviour and ability of the child concerned and any extra support which can be given. Usually an adult 'helper' or ancillary member of staff may be appointed to help the class teacher. This, then, is an outline of the various types of placements and provision available (depending on where you live). Provision varies from complete segregation to complete integration, and can depend on the child's individual needs and resources available.

Progress in Special Education: the Statement
In 1978 the *Warnock Report* was published. This was an important government report on children with special needs. It contains some 225 recommendations for children with special needs and recommends provision for children with special learning difficulties. It led to the 1981 Education Act, under which children are no longer to be labelled or classified by their disability. Instead, a 'statement' is made concerning the child and his needs, and parents are kept informed during the process.

Later Acts of 1988 and 1992 superceded the 1981 Education Act and in 1994 a Code of Practice was introduced. This clearly outlined the five stages to implement a school-based procedure towards making a Statement. Some children with special needs, which can be identified and assessed before admission to school, may already have a Statement when they start school.

All agencies concerned with the child's progress and development are required to submit assessments on the child's particular needs. The parents can see each one made. Such advice is required from the teacher, educational psychologist, medical officer and anyone else involved who has been working with and knows the child. The parents too are asked for their advice. All this information is then put together and a combined statement on the child's needs is produced. This will contain a recommendation for a suitable educational placement, where these needs can best be met. Parents are kept informed at each stage and a copy of the complete statement is sent to them. Parents now have a statutory right to a full say regarding both their child's needs and his placement, and have a right to choose the type of education from which they feel their child will most benefit.

When an educational placement has been recommended it is a good plan to contact the headteacher and Special Educational Needs Co-ordinator (SENCO) and ask if you can visit the school. Often you will be invited to do so. Do go along and meet the staff, who are usually very friendly and helpful. You can then see for yourself what the school is like and find out what kind of activities your child will be doing. If it is a school which caters for all ages – often the case with a special school – he may be there for the next eleven years! So do satisfy yourself that he will be happy there and able to benefit fully from the experience. Also, remember that your child may have to travel some distance. If so, most local authorities will arrange for transport to and from school.

The curriculum
The different kinds of educational provision which are likely to be encountered have already been outlined. The best option for the child will depend mainly on what is available and how the child will be able to cope. At the time of writing, children with Down's Syndrome are to be found in all forms of provision described. I feel strongly that the child's progress and achievement will hinge greatly on how much support parents are able to provide. These children thrive so much on praise, encouragement and plenty of individual help (as will any child!). If parents can give their child sufficient time and attention they will reinforce the learning skills acquired at school. They may be amazed at how quickly the child will learn and remember things – and it is good to see parents, teachers and carers working as a team.

Special education need not actually differ very much from main-stream education. One headmaster in a primary school said, after reading the aims of a special unit newly attached to his school, 'Yes, but these are aims which we hope to achieve with *all* our children.' Special Education does, however, look much more at the child's individual needs, and at all areas of his development. Having looked at, and assessed his development, an Individual Education Programme (IEP) can be set out. The aim is to help each child realise his full potential, and grow to become an independent and responsible young person.

Every child has an entitlement to the National Curriculum. Children

63

Tamsin, aged five, making music.

who are the subject of a Statement of Special Educational Needs will have their needs defined, the type of provision required to meet those needs and any additional resources which may be needed. All children will have access to the programmes of study as set out for the core subjects of English, Maths and Science and the foundation subjects of Design and Technology, Information Technology, History, Geography, Art, Music, Physical Education and, in senior schools, Modern Foreign Languages. There is also a legal requirement to teach Religious Education. Children are able to work at their own level of ability within each subject area and achieve their own levels of competence. Those who are slow or who experience some difficulty may have their own Individual Educational Programmes (IEP) and lesson planning will include differentiation in tasks to provide for differing levels of ability. Some lessons may be modified and (in rare cases) it may be felt that some requirements of the National Curriculum may be disapplied, either temporarily at the headteacher's discretion, or through the Statement. The Statement should also state if any areas of a developmental curriculum will apply and whether the child will benefit from any other resources such as those of a speech therapist.

Teachers hope to achieve all these aims by working through specific curriculum areas of development as discussed in the previous chapter. Each area can be developed and extended as the child progresses. Self-help skills are designed to help a child to become independent and responsible for himself socially and physically, so that he can care for himself and his own needs without adult interventio[n] should be able to get on well with others, to join in and to round. General behaviour and manners are important, b loping self-confidence and self-esteem and for being properly accepted.

Physical exercise and control are essential to the development of a fit, strong and healthy body. PE lessons, gym, athletics games and dancing or movement lessons all help to make limbs and body strong and well co-ordinated as well as to build self-confidence and social acceptability. Swimming, too, is valuable; not only does it help to tone the whole body and develop co-ordination, it has the added advantage of developing self-awareness and confidence which can spread positively into other areas of development and personality, often with far-reaching consequences.

The children need plenty of practice in finger movements and control. Any exercises or skills involving the use of fingers will help to improve this fine co-ordination. Different textures can be used to help train senses and promote fine finger control. Such activities may include playing with sand, water, paint, plasticine, pastry, chalk, crayons and felt pens and using scissors. Acquiring such skills can further assist the child to do things for himself just like other children, and again will boost self-confidence and social acceptability. A child will become much more independent when it can use scissors, paint, draw and write for itself – not to mention unscrewing jars, opening doors and turning switches on and off!

Communication may seem to be a problem area. Many children could be slow to develop language skills, or have a speech difficulty. Some children may be quite able to understand speech and written language but slow to respond, unwilling to reply, or behind in the development of their own expressive language. It is most frustrating for anyone not able to make themselves understood! Again, this is largely a developmental matter; given a stimulating environment with plenty of opportunity and encouragement all this will come in time. It develops through being able to listen and understand, to complete simple tasks and requests, carry out instructions, express thoughts, feelings and needs, and respond to the spoken word. Once these skills are learned the children should be encouraged to extend their vocabulary, their sentences and their thoughts.

These learning skills are ongoing and can be developed and ex-

James, aged seven, counting.

tended, step by small step, at every level. Cognitive ability, too, will grow as one activity leads on to another, increasing the understanding and awareness of the world around us, and the ability to use information. Placing and sorting objects will lead on to discovering the differences between shapes, colours and size. Handling toys and apparatus will stimulate language and number values such as counting, adding, taking away, recognising numbers, telling the time and handling money.

Recognising similar and different shapes, naming objects and pictures, enjoying books, stories and songs will spill over into reading activities; the child will discover that it can read for both meaning and pleasure. Being able to read and practise with pencil play – tracing and colouring – will develop handwriting skills.

Working with numbers, reading and writing, and doing things together can all result in finding out about the environment, what they can do and what other people do. This can build into project work and classroom activities so that the children will be discovering the new excitements of English, Maths, Science, Design Technology, Information Technology, History, Geography, Art, Music, Physical Education and Religious Education with access to the National Curriculum and work planned and differentiated for their level of ability.

Teaching aids
Schools as well as industry are moving further ahead into the age of technology. Computers are becoming widely used in all walks of life and in a variety of jobs. Education was quick to take up this challenge and has found that computers can be a valuable teaching and learning aid. More and more computers are finding their way into educational establishments at all levels from universities and colleges to senior, junior, infant and special schools, and also within schools for very disabled children. New software is being developed all the time. Computers have their place in special education too, providing a valuable adjunct to the curriculum and an additional resource. Information Technology is a requirement of the National Curriculum and all children have an entitlement and opportunity to use computers and to achieve their own level of capability. For children who have difficulty using the system available in their school there are various attachments that can be purchased to enable them to operate and to interact with the computer.

Other 'hardware' is widely used in schools these days, too. The television set has now been long established, and both BBC2 and Channel 4 produce and transmit regular programmes for all ages and

Laura, aged six, visiting Pets' Corner.

abilities, and keep abreast of the times by updating and producing innovative new programmes. A video recorder is a useful asset either used in conjunction with the television or on its own. Good TV programmes can be recorded and used again, but please ensure that you are not infringing any copyright regulations! The programme can be re-run, or a frame frozen while a teaching point is explained or discussed. If the school has a camcorder, too, or a digital camera, the educational potential of video is virtually endless. Filming the children in the classroom is a useful addition to a parents' meeting, or to note particular behaviour for assessment, as well as to stimulate the children and encourage their own expressive language. The children respond enthusiastically to seeing themselves in action. Video can be used to record visits, outings and classroom activities and can greatly help with language development as the children are stimulated to talk about what they have seen and done. They like to recognise people they know and usually have plenty to say! They will need encouragement to express themselves – but be prepared for the flood gates to open once they do!

Video, digital and polaroid cameras can produce instant action replay and immediate language stimulation. Ordinary cameras are very handy, too, whether using black and white film, colour prints or slides. A photo album to record school outings and activities will interest pupils and visitors alike.

Films, slides and overhead projectors can all be used to provide interest and variety to lessons and are again a useful aid to promote language development and discussion.

Radio programmes are also broadcast to schools; with the help of a tape recorder these can contribute variety and flexibility to the timetable. Cassettes offer a multitude of uses, and not only for recording and play back of programmes: I use cassettes as part of the reading scheme and read stories onto tapes to accompany the story books for the children to listen and follow. One of my pupils often chooses this for his bedtime story at home! Try to record the children reading and singing or telling their stories and news. They love to hear themselves and this will provide extra stimulation and attention. Parents can do all this at home, too. Familiar everyday noises can be recorded for children to recognise. Many of these ideas are now available commercially or through educational suppliers. However, tapes can always be made to suit individual requirements and interests, and you can have fun building up your own at home or school library. This should help in speech development too, as your child may well take extra care when it knows it is being recorded.

Listening to and recording the child's own voice can be extended by

James, aged seven, cooking.

the use of the Language Master. This system provides visual, hearing and speech stimulation while reinforcing reading activities. Record players and stereo equipment also have their place in schools and can provide music, story and song.

I find a computer keyboard a very valuable educational tool, too, especially once the children have started to read. The children in my care have learned to read faster than they can write. It is amazing how soon they find their way around the keyboard. They discover the use of the space bar and shift key in the first session. This can be a useful skill when using a computer. In the early stages self-adhesive labels with lower case letters can be placed on top of the capital letters, because the smaller letters will be learned and recognised first. These are also available commercially. This is a wonderful stimulus to motivate young children, since they love using anything mechanical; it provides a good reinforcer for visual recognition, sequencing, spacing and grammar. They very soon learn about capital letters and full stops!

These are the main items of aids and equipment used in schools for both teaching and assessment purposes. There are many other

Elizabeth, aged six, matching money.

teaching aids available too – for example, battery-operated educational apparatus and computer games which can be used both at home and at school.

The multi-disciplinary team

The specialist teacher in the special school, class or unit will not be working in isolation. Back-up support and team involvement are available to help with the development of each child. Some key people are regular visitors; others can be called in for advice as needed. Other professional agencies have already been described in the previous chapter and, if not already involved with the child, their services can be sought and contact maintained with the parents. The education, development and welfare of each child is the result of positive team effort. This team should include the parents, too. Each member of the team has a valuable contribution to make.

The teacher here is in a key position to keep the child under constant review. If the child is doing well then everyone can feel pleased. But if the teacher or the parents are concerned about some particular difficulty, additional support and advice is usually at the end of a

Katie, aged six, reading to Dylan.

telephone. Reassessment, consultations and case conferences usually form a regular part of the child's school education and can be arranged annually at the Review of the Statement or more frequently as and when needed.

The role of the parents

Parents may well be feeling by now that their child's future is no longer under their control – so many people offering advice and help could feel overwhelming! Nevertheless, you *are* still holding the reins. It is the parents who know their own child best. You are always present; you see him every day and get to know his ups and downs. You are usually the first to spot if something is not quite as it should be, and you can discuss this with the teacher or with any other agency who could help.

As a teacher, to work quite closely with the parents and family, I try to visit the home fairly regularly, and parents are always welcome to visit the school and spend half a day with us. We can talk about the children informally, share the many pleasures and make the best out of the not-so-good patches. My parents can come along and help in the classroom and watch the teaching methods used. There is often more than one way of doing something, and an alternative may be better suited to a particular individual.

The support they are willing to give to the child will depend a lot on how much they expect from him themselves. I find that most parents are very supportive once they understand how important it is to give their special child plenty of attention, and to reinforce the skills learned in school, and to try and do the same things in a similar way at home.

One very important point, already mentioned, is to treat the child as a normal little boy or girl. Do not expect too little from them, or you will only get a little in return. If you expect your child to behave like a normal child you will be more than halfway there; it will rise to the occasion and respond to your positive attitude. The self-fulfilling prophecy really does work! Children instinctively know exactly how much you want from them. They know that you are expecting them to behave in a silly or babyish way and be naughty they will do so. If you, expect them to behave sensibly and in a well-mannered way they will respond accordingly. Remember the children who rushed to fetch a chair and open the door? – you too will find that sowing the seeds in the early years will help you reap the rewards later.

Checklist: Starting school

1. General readiness

Pre-school visit

Can he

listen and understand	_____
sit on toilet	_____
wash hands	_____
feed himself	_____
place coat on peg	_____
help to undress/dress himself	_____
feel happy as a member of a group	_____
learn a routine	_____
fetch and replace articles	_____
share, and wait his turn	_____
get on with adults and children	_____

2. Placement and provision

Can you visit a

normal school	_____
Special School	_____
Special Unit attached to school	_____

Will he need

transport	_____
ancillary help	_____
professional help	_____
any special aids (which)	_____

Note: how well can the school provide for children with Special Educational Needs?

3. Teaching aids

Check equipment available

Computer	_____
Television	_____
Video	_____
Radio	_____
Camera	_____
Cassette recorder and player	_____

Language Master   _____
CD player   _____

---

4. Parental role and rights

Statement issued on your child

Has one been issued?   _____
Are you being kept fully
  informed?   _____
Signified your agreement/
  disagreement?   _____
Satisfied with statement as to
  needs?   _____
Satisfied with proposed provision? _____
Involved in annual review?   _____
Been invited to join in
  consultation?   _____
Met with the SENCO?   _____

Regular review and assessment

Arrangements in hand?   _____

Regular check-ups

Paediatrician   _____
Optician/ophthalmologist   _____
Audiometrician (ears)   _____
School medical (date?)   _____
Speech therapist   _____

Other

Encouraging independence in
  your child   _____
Seeking help and advice when
  needed   _____
Offering support to the school   _____

4
Handing over the Reins: A Shared Responsibility for Parents, Teachers and Carers

Meeting other professionals

Children with Down's Syndrome will come into contact with many other people during their lives. Initially many of these will be with the Health Service and then the Education Service and Social Services. The parents and child will meet many of these people for consultation and advice on health, development and educational aspects for the child.

Hospital staff – midwife, nurses, paediatrician and perhaps a social worker – are the first to meet with new parents and will be in a position to discuss the condition and needs of the child and offer support. The immediate family, friends and relations will be the next to meet the baby and can provide comfort and support.

When the baby arrives home and becomes a member of his new family he will be seen regularly by the health visitor, family doctor (GP), and staff at the health centre or baby clinic where he will be taken for routine visits and check-ups. Parents will have the opportunity to meet with other parents, young children and professionals and be able to share experiences and expertise. New ideas or those already tried and tested are always welcome! There may also be a parent and toddler group in your area for pre-school children with special needs, or a local branch of the Down's Syndrome Association or Mencap, and a Child Development Centre where clinics are held by professionals in their particular specialism. These clinics will most likely include speech therapy, physiotherapy, occupational therapy, hearing assessment, vision assessment and a regular review with the paediatrician. Support and advice can be given and problems shared.

Contact the Social Services too, as playgroups, holiday schemes, link families and respite care can be arranged, depending on the needs of

76

your child and your family. Friends and relations can also provide welcome support and relief and will probably be pleased to offer a babysitting service. Parents need some time to themselves and a break from the constant care and demands of caring for a young child and family, especially when they have a child with special needs – and help is available!

Advice and support

Soon parents will be meeting with the educational psychologist, community nurse or Portage worker. They can arrange to assess the child's development and behaviour and can provide regular help and advice to develop the young child's skills and abilities so that parents and family members can work with the child at home. This will give a young child with Down's Syndrome a valuable early start in learning how to do things for itself and in learning socially acceptable behaviour so that it can begin to become a valued member of its family and to gain skills to help it to achieve his full potential. It will also help tremendously when the child starts school.

Many of the professionals mentioned so far will often have students with them. Nearly all students, during the course of their studies, will have a practical placement for 'on the job experience'. We are all working together to learn from each other and to help each other.

Up to this point, most of the help which parents and children receive will seem to be in an advisory capacity. However, the next step will be to plan an opportunity for the young child to attend a pre-school provision. This may be for young children with special educational needs, for average ability children or a provision for both. Special needs provision may be a pre-school group at a child development centre or in a diagnostic and assessment unit. Other provision may be in a playgroup or a nursery. These may be organised by the local education authority (LEA), a charity group or church, or run privately. The staff and helpers should be qualified as nursery nurses or nursery teachers, or have a playgroup diploma or other revelant qualifications. Parents can visit with their child before admission and are usually welcome to stay for a while. This can ensure that everyone has met each other and all are happy with the arrangements. Special needs provisions usually have a good ratio of helpers as it is recognised that children with special needs require a lot of individual help. If parents discuss the placements and their child's needs with the educational psychologist or social worker they will probably find that some additional support can be provided for their child, e.g. an ancillary helper. As the child is still very young he may be attending only on a part-time basis – a full week can be extremely tiring for very young children! Parents may also find that a special school has its own nursery class or is able to take pupils from an early age (2–3 years), or the local infant or primary school may have a nursery or under-fives class where children can attend part time until they are five (the statutory age for full-time education).

First steps away from home

By now our young children with Down's Syndrome could be attending pre-school assessment classes, nursery, playgroup, school or holiday play schemes or be receiving respite care. Sooner or later we all have to hand our children over to other carers for the greater part of any day. If the child has to travel any distance to 'school', transport may be arranged by the LEA. This should be discussed with the educational psychologist who will be able to make the necessary arrangements. The child will then be in the care of the taxi driver who will usually have an escort to take care of the child on the journey. Parents will naturally wish to reassure themselves that their child is in 'safe hands' and being well taken care of. Ideally, all carers, teachers and staff will by now have visited and talked with parents and children, and come to know about the child's personality and ability.

How do we help?

'What do I do? How do I treat him?' asked my new taxi escort after we had all met. 'Just like anyone else. Like any child you look after. Like your own children.' was the prompt reply. But, at the same time, being aware of the child's special needs or learning difficulties! Help the child to help himself – don't do it for him when he can do something for himself. Encourage self-help skills, independence and responsibility for himself and his possessions at all times. Support and encourage him to become a little person in his own right. And praise for effort as well as achievement. We all thrive on praise and attention. Give it for good behaviour – then attention will not be given so frequently for non-acceptable behaviour. Children like to be noticed. In fact, they demand attention! They will soon learn how to get it for unacceptable behaviour – children with Down's Syndrome are no exception to this rule!

Behaviour problems or not

The biggest problem which all teachers and all carers have with children is bad behaviour – and how to cope with it. As well as distracting other members of the class or group, unacceptable behaviour patterns detract from the effectiveness of the activity and the overall management. This is not to say that all children with Down's Syndrome are naughty or badly behaved, any more or less than any other children of the same age. In fact, to be naughty is sometimes quite 'normal' behaviour at any age! One of my own pupils with Down's Syndrome was very well behaved, obedient and hardworking. So the first day that she played up and did something that was unacceptable and needed reprimanding and correcting we almost cheered because she was showing perfectly normal behaviour! On the other hand, there were two pupils who were habitually 'naughty' and constantly receiving attention for unacceptable behaviour. This problem can arise from time to time. When we see it emerging it is important to attempt to stop any bad behaviour, naughtiness or silliness before it gets out of control and becomes a game or routine. Most importantly, the child himself needs to learn how to behave appropriately, to develop age-appropriate behaviour alongside his peers, so that he can become acceptable within society.

Start as you mean to go on! Try to stop it – explain that 'we do not do that here'. Distract the child: 'That's not very nice. Let's come over here and try this.' Try to be positive and not negative: 'Let's do it like this, good, well done!' Give praise and reward for good behaviour or a task well done. Fade plenty of initial praise and practical rewards so that praise becomes more relevant and verbal praise becomes the only necessary reward over a period of time. Ignore minor occurrences (if possible!) as long as there is no possible danger to people or things. Children dislike being ignored, and why continue doing something if it does not get the desired effect? Enlist peer group support. For example, if Johnny finds it difficult to sit still during story time – when you are sitting next to him, just remind him quietly to sit still and listen so that all can hear. Involve the class in making their own rules which they can all help each other to keep.

Expectations

Have high expectations! (But make sure that they are realistic too.) If you aim high the child will respond to the best of its ability. If you aim low it will make less effort. Teachers do not mind if a child has difficulty with a task as long as it is making an effort, or performing within its own level of ability; at least it is making an attempt. What is frustrating is when a child is making no attempt, especially when we know that he can do something! If it is not attending to the task it is more likely to 'do its own thing' and get into mischief or distract others from working to the best of their ability. Again, praise for effort as well as achievement. A little praise goes a long way.

Scott, aged nine, sailing.

Support for learning

All children learn. All children need help to learn. They are learning all the time, in any situation and in any environment, whether at home, school, leisure or being cared for. Learning will not take place until you have established eye contact with the child and engaged its attention and focused it on the task in hand. The attention span (time) may be limited at first but will grow with interest and achievement. Whether helping the child with Down's Syndrome to acquire development skills or achieve targets set within the Statement, or pursuing programmes of study within the National Curriculum, it will need a lot more help and support to practise, learn, reinforce and use its skills. The child needs to listen attentively and understand clearly explained steps and directions. These may need to be broken down into smaller steps to reach a target. Can he hear adequately? Is there a confusing background noise? Can he see well enough to perform a task? Is he able to see the teacher's face when she is talking? The blackboard? His helper? Is the lighting adequate in the room? Is he sitting in the shade? Is there a glare on the computer screen? Is he sitting comfortably? If the task is new the child may need very close individual help, explanation in detailed steps, physical patterning (e.g. pencil skills) and plenty of practice to become proficient. As he learns to perform a task, give him a degree of independence, encourage him to do things for himself – when and as much as he can.

The child's welfare

While the child is in the care of others it will be supervised at all times. The degree of individual support it receives will depend on its own degree of personal skill and independence, whether supervised personally or within the group or class. The aim is always to foster supported independence in all skills and activities from personal needs of toileting, washing, dressing, feeding, playing, through to subject areas of the National Curriculum and at playtimes.

Towards a level of independence

Above all, give each child a chance to do things for himself. Let him have opportunities and experiences. 'Let's have a go.' 'Let's try it.' Give him a chance to show what he can learn and what he can do. He will respond to a routine – he will learn within it. He needs to find his boundaries, how far he can go and what he can do. He will respond to consistency, kindness, firmness, attention and praise for his efforts and achievements, so growing in his own self-confidence and self-esteem.

This can only be achieved when all people concerned, parents, teachers and carers, work together as a team, to help each other to help the child. The parents know their child best of all, they have had him since birth, they have the full-time care and responsibility. Teachers and carers come in to work with parents to help and support the child. We are all helping the child to help himself.

Checklist: A shared responsibility

1. Professionals

Midwife	_____
Paediatrician	_____
GP	_____
Health visitor	_____
Social worker	_____
Educational psychologist	_____
Community nurse	_____
Portage worker	_____
Nursery nurse	_____
Teacher	_____

2. Clinics

Baby clinic	_____
Mother and Baby group	_____
Toddler group	_____
Child development centre	_____
Speech therapy	_____
Physiotherapy	_____
Occupational therapy	_____
Hearing	_____
Vision	_____
Paediatrician review	_____

3. Social Services

Respite care	_____
Link families	_____
Holiday play scheme	_____

4. Pre-school groups

Child development centre
Down's Syndrome Association _____
Mencap _____
Diagnostic and assessment unit _____
Playgroup
Nursery
Under-fives class _____

5. School

Infant
Junior _____
Special unit _____
Special school _____
Private school _____

6. Carers

Parents _____
Teachers _____
Ancillary _____
Taxi escort _____
Babysitter _____
Play scheme _____
Link family _____
Respite care _____
Family members _____

7. How to help

Treat as normal _____
Give attention _____
Divert or fade bad behaviour _____
Praise effort and results _____
Offer a reward _____

Peer group support   _____
High realistic expectations _____

---

8. Learning skills

Attention to task   _____
Eye contact   _____
Hear well   _____
See well   _____
Understand clearly   _____
Comfortable   _____
Small steps   _____
Physical patterning   _____
Healthy and well   _____
Level of independence   _____
Working together   _____

5
The Door of Opportunity: What Will the Future Hold?

Milestones

As we progress through life, whatever troubles it holds for us, we continue to develop and mature, as does our attitude to our fellow beings. For children with Down's Syndrome, who need many a helping hand on their way, each small step is an important achievement, and should be rewarded with loving praise and encouragement. This in its turn develops a vital sense of self-worth and individual pride. Each little step represents a milestone, and can lead to greater things.

I had been taking a group of children swimming regularly for about eighteen months. They enjoyed these sessions immensely. The three boys soon took to the water and were quite at home in the shallow paddling pool where they had confidence to jump in, splash, kick, swim with their face in the water and turn on their back. Indeed, they could have been any little boys enjoying themselves. However, they had a natural reserve and resisted going into the deep pool, clinging like a limpet to the adult with them. It was with great difficulty that we each managed to prise off four tightly clinging limbs and encourage them to splash about in the water while we held on. As they gained confidence they still would not leave the adult, but finally it just needed the token reassurance of a finger under their arm to help them 'swim' across the pool.

Swimming sessions are great fun. We were playing together one afternoon when, suddenly, the children were able to swim between us right across the pool, without the adult support so desperately needed before. A great noisy cheer went up! The other swimmers must have thought we were having a gala. It certainly felt like it! They had *each* achieved a personal success and, so pleased with themselves, have never looked back. At my instigation some delightful swimming certificates were designed by one of my helpers to mark the occasion and duly

Christopher, aged ten, using the computer.

presented by the headteacher in assembly. For the children themselves this was an enormous boost to self-confidence and independence, and it has visibly spilled over into other areas – there is just no holding them now!

I remember one little boy who was scared stiff of the large climbing apparatus in the gym when he first arrived, and in the same way clung to the adult helper. Twelve months later I heard a shout from the other side of the hall, 'Look at me!' I duly turned round to find him hanging upside down four feet off the ground. These are just a few examples of the many rewards gained through patience and perseverance, continual praise and encouragement. But, again, the most important achievement is the child's own self-esteem: he can do things just like anyone else. Similarly the little five-year-old girl who can do up the buckle on her sandal: she doesn't need any help. 'I do it *myself*,' she tells you crossly. Well done!

86

Towards eleven

As the child approaches the age of eleven further thought will be given to the next stage of education. If his needs are being met within an all-age school, as many special schools are, there will be an opportunity to progress into the senior department. Here the curriculum will embody a wider range of activities and experiences. In all types of educational provision, an annual assessment and review will be made on the child's progress and suitability of placement. Indeed, after the Education Acts of 1981, 1988 and 1992, and the Code of Practice of 1994, this is now required by law. Remember, too, that parents will still have their say. They can agree to the suitable placement of the child, or disagree if they are unhappy about it. It is possible to change the educational placement if the child's needs can best be met elsewhere, provided such facilities are available. Children placed in a junior unit or mainstream school will most likely be able to move onto a senior unit or mainstream school. The teachers who work with the child will be in a position to offer guidance and advice.

Post-sixteen

Nor does education automatically stop at sixteen (the statutory minimum school-leaving age). In fact, these days wider educational opportunities are available to almost everyone, in any walk of life, and at any age depending on their ability and interests. Many adults in the 'normal' community attend evening classes in all kinds of subjects for self-improvement or leisure, or they enrol at colleges of further education or study with the Open University. Many re-train to change jobs. The possibilities, and the reasons, are endless.

But what of our children? What will the future hold in store for them? Many parents have expressed concern over their youngsters continuing education especially as, previously, it seemed to come to an abrupt end with the doors closed at sixteen. Many of our children who had been learning very slowly were just beginning to get somewhere. Their parents felt, and knew, that given the opportunity they would be able to develop further. But what could they do?

It was under such conditions, some years ago, that one particular Further Education Unit was set up through a parents' pressure group. This Unit was planned so that the school-leavers could attend both the Further Education Unit and the adult training centre part-time during the next three years. This way they could benefit from part-time further education, according to their needs, whilst attending the training centre to which they later moved full time. Here they would have supervised employment. I have watched many of these young people develop a feeling of responsibility and grow in independence, able to find their own way around the community. They can all be trained to learn to catch a bus from their own home and get off at the bus station, cross the road and get to school or college by themselves. One young lad with Down's Syndrome, aged seventeen, was able to take a bus from home, change in the city centre, where he caught another bus to take him to the swimming pool. He got off, crossed another busy main road, entered the pool, paid his admission, changed and enjoyed his swim. Afterwards he was able to find his way home again. He was a perfectly responsible member of the community!

Some special schools now provide post-sixteen education courses for their pupils, still within the school. Certain colleges of further education provide courses within the college for special needs students who can attend various courses provided for them, with the opportunity of integrating with selected courses and meeting other students socially. This depends a lot on how the college is organised and what facilities are available – also, of course, on how well the particular individual will cope. Opportunities, then, may be found to continue with education beyond the usual school-leaving age.

Preparation for life
As the next step, preparing to leave school, looms in sight, questions will be asked again. What will he do when he leaves school? Indeed, there are many more possibilities than had once been thought. Many have opened the doors of opportunity, and left them open for a new generation to follow. Education is often regarded as a preparation for life; the senior department will be planning a curriculum to suit these needs that can be rational, relevant and realistic, while still meeting the individual needs of their young pupils and providing access to the National Curriculum.

The aim will be to widen their experiences and extend their activities within the original structure of the five basic areas of development we have discussed, as well as teaching life skills and gaining qualifications. They will progress through shorter steps and pass many smaller goals along the way. As always, one assesses the situation, in this case the child's development so far, and plans ahead, teaching the next step or few steps with the long-term goal in sight. Each area of development – communication, social ability, physical skills, self-help skills and cognitive ability – are important in their own right. Taken together they represent a picture of the child's all-round development and well-being. These areas naturally develop alongside each other and overlap.

Even if a youngster cannot speak very well, has difficulty in walking, a problem with dressing or cannot read, he can still become socially acceptable, and learn how to behave well. (Can we say that of all teenagers?) Training him how to conduct himself when out will help everyone, none more so than the child himself. One of my pupils was recently taken out for a meal for a family celebration in a restaurant. As usual, he was polite, well-mannered and ate his meal beautifully – unlike his sisters who failed to rise to the occasion. This was a result of a combination of social training (going out together) and self-help skills (feeding himself), and knowing how to behave and what was expected of him (social skills).

Socially children with Down's Syndrome need more practice in getting along with other people, in learning how to behave and how to do things for themselves and other people. But this experience all contributes towards being accepted by others. Finding their way around the neighbourhood is helpful, too; they discover where the local shops are and what they sell, where the Post Office, library and police station are, where to catch a bus, how to use a public telephone, where to post a letter and how to go on a shopping errand. At school and at home the children can learn how to make visitors welcome, deliver messages, help at meal times, do some simple cooking, use a hammer or screwdriver, make useful and attractive objects with all kinds of craft and DIY materials, play card and board games together, make their own beds, help with the cleaning, wash the car and help in the garden.

Many of these activities develop self-help skills. Let him try to do as much as possible for himself, even if he does need to be shown; if a particular skill needs to be broken down into smaller steps teach it by 'backward chaining'. Push him gently towards being an independent young person; discreetly withdraw your own physical support as he gains confidence in his own ability. Supervise from a distance until you are sure that he is responsible. Let him fetch his own toys and books; let him replace them when he has finished and help to tidy up afterwards.

Social competence and independence do hinge on the ability to express oneself adequately. It is usually recognised that most children with Down's Syndrome are a little slow in their speech and language development. If speech is very much delayed or presents special difficulties, early forms of communication should involve the use of gestures and signs, to recognise and express meaning. But this is perfectly natural among all young children, as a means of making their needs understood or to express their feelings, and precedes speech itself. Some schools with provision for children with severe communication difficulties do make use of various forms of sign language. The ones generally in use are the Makaton sign language and Bliss symbolics which are used along with normal speech. People in contact with these children usually need to know how to use it, too. Teachers, staff and parents will all be taught how to use and communicate with the sign language or communication system in use.

As normal patterns of speech develop, attention must be given to the meaning and understanding of first the spoken and then the written word. It is meaningless if the child does not understand the vocabulary used and has learned parrot-fashion without comprehension. This is why it pays to use speech with activities, indeed with anything you do, so that understanding and awareness of meaning can grow. Play with the child, and get him to follow out simple instructions such as 'Put the doll in the car', 'Put the plate on the table', 'Give me a cup and a spoon'.

Later on the child will be able to 'Go into the garden and tell daddy that dinner is ready' – three directions, garden, daddy and dinner. Eventually he may be able to respond to 'Put on your coat, take this note and money, and go down the road to the shop. Ask Mrs Baker if you can have some milk, tea and sugar please.' Then, he may be able to come back and make a cup of tea for you! Obviously, a lot of preparation will have been done to achieve this, but if he has had plenty of experience in helping you in each of these tasks he will know and understand what to do.

Carrying messages, whether written or verbal, involves the need to move around. Unless there is some particular disability all children with Down's Syndrome will be able to walk, run, jump and climb just as others do. Playing games, football, cricket, climbing in the gym, dancing to music, swimming, riding a bicycle may be included at school and can be a part of family life too. Strong healthy bodies, and the development of physical skills will greatly foster self-confidence. Many of these skills promote social attributes as well and enable the child to join in with family and friends.

Fine-finger co-ordination can present a difficulty, but practice in fine-finger movements and attention to detail will help. This can involve all kinds of activities from scribbling, tracing, colouring, to writing, using a computer, scissors, paint brush, needle and thread, pressing buttons on a cassette or other machines, mixing dough, rolling and cutting pastry and placing on a baking tray, laying the table, preparing vegetables for dinner, spreading butter and cutting cakes, washing and drying dishes, using tools and helping daddy. All help to develop fine-finger co-ordination as well as other worthwhile skills resulting in increased personal independence and social competence.

All these activities are likely to form part of the normal routine within a senior department at school, so extending the child's experience and awareness of the world in which he lives. Television programmes, films, visits and topic work within the National Curriculum will add enrichment so that the children will be finding out and discovering things that are natural, historical, geographical, artistic, creative, scientific, healthy and spiritual, developing their own awareness and understanding of the world. Basic work in reading, writing and maths will continue at their own pace at the same time.

The final year or so as the children approach sixteen is usually organised on a practical basis to prepare them for leaving school and to become more independent and responsible. Many units and schools include craft areas for activities such as sewing, woodwork and pottery, and very often a kitchen, dining room or flat where they can learn how to keep house, entertain others, and look after themselves. These skills are carefully taught and the young people can learn how to live with a degree of independence both in home and work situations. It is at this point that we are more likely to witness the main results of education for children with special needs – fulfilment of potential as independent and responsible young persons within the community. And, as one headmaster of a mainstream junior school said, that after all is what we would wish for *all* our children. As to the level of achievement and ability reached, this will depend closely on the amount of time, help and understanding and encouragement that can be given.

They will also be able to progress at their own pace and level of ability through the Key Stages of the National Curriculum, achieving their own levels of ability and competence and, like peers, sitting the SATS (Standard Attainment Tests) at 7, 11 and 14 years.

Their future in your hands
The activities and experiences received at school can all be practised and reinforced at home within the family circle. The education of the child should be a rewarding partnership between home and school, the two agencies most closely concerned with the child's well-being during the vital years of development. Sharing experiences between the family and school should now be a natural part of your life together. Your child may even yet be running down the road to ask Mrs Baker for the sugar, tea and milk, or making you that welcome cup of tea when you collapse into a chair exhausted at the end of a busy day.

You will, of course, have accompanied him to the shop from his earliest days, in the push-chair at first, next on the reins and then tightly clutching his hand. Later you will be able to let him walk in a controlled way sensibly beside you. Choose one item for him to find in the shop first; let him find it, take it to the checkout and ask or pay for it. Later on he can find some new things. If the shop is just down the road and within sight of your doorstep this would be very convenient! On the other hand, you may need to cross a busy main road or the shop may be out of sight around the corner, in which case you'll need to gauge the advisability of such an expedition. But you may be able to go with him to the corner, let him go into the shop on his own and meet him when he comes out. He may even have an obliging elder brother or sister who will watch him part way or walk down the road with him first, so that he knows it is all right without you. Do talk to him and praise him so that he knows what is expected of him, and knows that he will be rewarded on his safe return.

Your teenager may be able to catch a bus on his own to change a library book, visit Auntie (or go for a swim like our other young man!). If you feel that such adventures are possible, that you have already made plenty of such trips together and that you are ready to trust him, let him have a go. He will never be able to do it unless you give him the chance to try – even if it means Auntie meeting him off the bus or, later, watching for him from her gate. Or, perhaps, you will discreetly follow him in the car having put him safely on the bus first!

A teacher friend of mine taught a young student to catch the bus by herself in just such a way. First she drove her car to the bus stop and put her safely on the bus, then followed in her car and met her when she got off. She can now make the trip by herself unaided. Her mother had said she could never do it! Let's always try to foster self-confidence in our young people, and lead them towards being independent. Perhaps the parents need their own confidence boosted, too! I sincerely hope that you too reach this stage – it will prove just how much your youngster, and you, have achieved.

Let your son or daughter take on their share of the responsibilities for family chores. They will know, and be able to feel, that they are a valued member of the family, helping to prepare meals and clean up afterwards, answer the door or the telephone, hold the wood and screws for that extra shelf and use the hammer and screwdriver, too. One mum I know was lying in bed with a bad back and her thirteen-year-old daughter made her some tea and toast. 'Here you are, Mummy!' she said. Mum expressed her thanks and appreciation and duly praised her daughter, to be immediately rewarded with a characteristic and effusive bear hug in response which hurt her back even more! Depending on your own family interests and circumstances you will best know how you can actively involve your son or daughter. One father confided to me that one day soon he hopes to take his son to the local pub, and that his son will stand him a drink.

Quality of life

As fully paid up members of family and school these young people should be busy in leading not only a happy life, but one that is both purposeful and meaningful. What can the child look forward to? Depending on his own success to date, he can expect a measure of independence and responsibility both towards himself and towards others. There will be many things he can do to give him security, boost his morale, and enable him to take a justifiable pride in himself and his own particular skills.

In order to reach this degree of independence much will depend on the amount of time and effort which you as a parent as well as teachers, are prepared to give the child. During the years at school, education will play a valuable part, and many other members of the professional team may be able to help and advise too, so contributing towards the child's progress and general well-being. But the parents are there from the start; those early pre-school years are valuable for any child, and how much more so for the toddler with Down's Syndrome? Those years are widely recognised as a key stage of formative growth, if the child is going to benefit fully from attending school. I have seen children respond to new activities and progress at a pleasing rate secure in the knowledge of their parents' approval, support and stimulation. Others, with exactly the same potential and enthusiasm have achieved less, for want of the right support at home. A teacher's time and energy are necessarily limited by the hours in a school day, extra activities on the timetable, and the demands of the other children in her care. Parents are always there to give encouragement and praise and create a new diversion. *Your* child needs *you*.

Opening the door

Progress in attitudes towards the learning disabled members of our community has been slow. But, in recent years, alongside the publication of the *Warnock Report* and the subsequent Education Acts, attitudes are changing. Fear and prejudice are of course still to be found around us, as in so many other aspects of society; but more is being done to educate the public as to the nature of the problems and the potential which exists. Our children are living in a remarkable new age with more possibilities and more understanding than ever before. Given half a chance they will be able to show us that they are individuals in their own right – and *with* their own rights – and that they too can learn to handle a learning disability which is after all secondary to the unique experience of human life and individual personality.

What of the future? What choice can there be for a young adult with Down's Syndrome, within our society? Hitherto the choice has been limited. Many parents chose to keep their young adult at home and to care for him themselves. But for those who have led a sheltered life in a protective environment, another problem may arise when the parents themselves become elderly and can no longer manage a special needs son or daughter, unused to looking after themselves and knowing no other environment. It is then felt to be cruel to uproot them from their only known home and place them with strangers – a dilemma, indeed, and one arising from the best of intentions.

Others have been fortunate enough to carry on living at home but able to go out each day to spend some time profitably at a day centre, adult training centre or sheltered workshop. Here they have been able to meet socially with other people and supervisors and perhaps start earning a wage.

With luck, suitable hostel provision may be found where both young and older adults can stay on a permanent or a part-time basis, the latter enabling them to spend some time at home. This can also ease the situation later on, should it ever become impractical to keep the special needs member at home; he will then have somewhere to go where he is already known and with which he himself is familiar. He may also be able to visit an adult training centre, sheltered workshop or local job from the hostel.

In some areas hostel provision can be arranged based on individual or shared flats or bed-sits; here a degree of independence can be maintained while the youngster remains under the overall care and supervision of a warden. There are also village communities specially designed to care for people with learning disabilities where they can play a full part in community life and work.

The emphasis these days, whenever funds are available, is on creating housing and hostel provision offering a degree of independence and the chance to go out and work, go shopping, take part in local activities, visit friends and receive visitors.

There are some training schemes which prepare the young adult for work experience whereby he can continue to live at home, in a hostel or a community, but still have the opportunity to go out to work. More places are provided at colleges of further education. The students attend courses to suit their needs and interests with opportunities to integrate into college life and activities. They can work and study to gain qualifications and receive support in finding work experience and placements and in learning on-the-job skills. I know of one young adult who received training in this way and is now happy and busy working as a gardener and doing very well. Opportunities for work will vary a lot from one area to another, but teachers, social workers and training scheme organisers will be able to advise parents when the time comes.

There is no need – or excuse – these days for children or young people to be put away or hidden from society, forgotten and neglected. They are individual people with something to offer and a role in life to play. The future is an unknown path for all of us. Who knows what tomorrow may bring? But the future is theirs. There is a new generation of children with Down's Syndrome growing up today who are profiting from realistic ideas and supported by forward-looking educational methods and expertise. They have as much right to a happy, fulfilling and rewarding life as anyone. I am convinced that they are ready to show us what they can do. Let's open the doors and make every use of the opportunities before us.

Many of these children, whom I count myself fortunate to know, never cease to amaze me, and thrill their parents, by showing what they can do. If they can achieve, why shouldn't others do so too? Unfortunately, we can still hear people saying, 'They won't be able to to this,' or 'They'll never be able to do that.' Why ever not? They have already exploded many myths. They can learn and they *do* learn – and they will show us! For myself, I no longer say, 'No, they can't,' instead I say, 'Let's have a go, we'll try.' I know they will surprise us all by their capabilities and skills. Open the door, seize the opportunity; the future may well be theirs, but it will be one for you to share and enjoy, too.

Checklist: Development for life

1. Social

Relates well to peers and adults	_____
Can find his way around home and school	_____
Behaviour is socially acceptable	_____
Can run messages	_____

Able to join youth clubs and take
   part in community activities   _____
Behaves well on school/family trips _____

2. Communication

Can express his needs and feelings _____
Can be understood by others   _____
Greets people   _____
Describes what he has been doing _____
Goes shopping   _____
Delivers messages   _____
Uses telephone   _____
Chooses TV programmes   _____

3. Self-help

Handles personal needs
   (toilet, washing, dressing,
   eating)   _____
Makes own bed   _____
Tidies own room   _____
Can cook simple meals   _____
Can wash dishes and clothes   _____

4. Cognitive

Reading level   Uses flash cards   _____
                  Has social sight vocabulary _____
                  Reads for pleasure   _____
                  Reads for information   _____

Writing   Signs own name   _____
                  Writes name and address   _____
                  Writes short story or own news _____
                  Writes and sends birthday cards _____
                  Writes and sends Christmas cards _____
                  Writes thankyou notes   _____

Numeracy level   Counts and recognises numbers
         up to 6   _____
Plays dice, card and board games   _____
Adds and subtracts numbers up
         to 10   _____
Adds and subtracts numbers up
         to 20   _____
Recognises numbers up to 100   _____
Knows most coin values   _____
Knows all coin values   _____
Goes into shop on his own   _____
Can count change   _____
Can work out change from £1, etc. _____
Tells the time in hours   _____
Tells the time in half hours   _____
Tells the time in quarter hours   _____
Knows 'It is nearly/just
         gone . . . o'clock'   _____

---

5. Gross motor ability

He can   Walk   _____
Run   _____
Ride a bicycle   _____
Use a bus and car   _____
Play ball games   _____
Swim   _____
Go shopping   _____
Visit local amenities   _____
Attend youth club/evening classes _____
Perform household chores   _____
Attend to garden tasks   _____
Care for family pet   _____

---

6. Fine motor ability

He can   Trace   _____
Colour   _____
Use pen/pencil to write or draw   _____

Use scissors _____

Use a knife, fork and spoon _____

Press switches and buttons _____

Use a needle and thread _____

7. Further education and training

An enormous number of courses and classes are becoming available today.

Check

Local Education Office _____

Public library _____

College of further education _____

School _____

Evening class centres _____

Down's Syndrome Association _____

Home Farm Trust _____

Mencap _____

8. Investigative leisure activities

Youth clubs _____

Sports/leisure centres _____

Gym/health clubs _____

Swimming _____

Reading _____

Horse-riding _____

Cycling _____

Dancing _____

Crafts (great variety) _____

Card and board games _____

Library _____

Visits and outings _____

Trips away _____

Holiday centres _____

Gardening _____

Theme parks _____

9. Maturity for life

Is he ready for: Working at home   _____
Taking up local employment   _____
Joining a college course   _____
Going on a residential course   _____
Joining a sheltered workshop   _____
Joining a day centre   _____
Joining an adult training centre   _____
Living in a hostel   _____
Making a home in the community   _____
Joining the Home Farm Trust   _____

10. Steps to independence

Can he   Catch the bus   _____
Go shopping   _____
Cook   _____
Make his own bed   _____
Tidy up his room   _____
Wash   _____
Clean the house   _____
Do some gardening   _____
Use the library   _____
Use the Post Office   _____
Use the telephone   _____
Entertain his friends   _____
Drive a car   _____

6
The Ultimate Responsibility

The birth of a baby with Down's Syndrome is bound to produce mixed reactions, among the new parents, as well as close friends and relatives. Initial reactions will vary considerably and feelings will oscillate between complete acceptance and total rejection, between a desire to protect and to abandon. These emotions are perfectly normal and need to be discussed, shared and overcome during this early period of adjustment. Feelings of guilt and blame also need to be dealt with; it is not the parents' fault, but they will need to come to terms with a native fear and prejudice in others, however well-meaning they may be.

These attitudes towards members of our community with learning disabilities can still persist, although it must be said they usually arise through fear and ignorance. After the birth of a second child one mother was asked by an unthinking acquaintance about her first child (who had Down's Syndrome: 'What will you do with him now?' Luckily public attitudes are improving, especially when these children and young people take their place in the community and thus come to be known for *who* they are and not what they are.

Many of their so-called 'normal' counterparts have their full share of problems and disabilities. Each of us is an individual personality in our own right. Each of us develops according to inherited characteristics and environmental factors within the home, school and community. At least parents of children with Down's Syndrome are aware of their child's condition almost from the start – unlike other disabilities which may not be revealed until a later date or suddenly arise through illness or accident.

All babies have similar basic needs which must be met. They have normal feelings and reactions, too. Black or white, healthy or sick, girl or boy, all need love and security, feeding, warmth, bathing, dressing, sleep, company and stimulation, within a warm and loving family atmosphere. A little dose of tender loving care can go a long way. The baby too will learn more quickly to respond and to express himself. The baby with Down's Syndrome will progress, like any other child, along recognised patterns of normal development, but usually at a much slower pace. He will require plenty of help and encouragement, but he will progress, step by step. However small the steps in between may be, visible milestones will be reached and passed. Both parents and child will be rewarded through plenty of praise and encouragement. Enjoy your baby and treat him as a normal person and as a rightful member of the family.

Shared responsibilities
At first many new parents may well feel isolated in their task, which may seem enormous, even daunting, in its aspect. They will look around for advice and support. This, too, may seem to be unforthcoming or difficult to find. But help certainly *is* available to those who seek it. Specialist services are, however, not made available automatically and the right channels of communiation between hospital, NHS Trust, social services and the education system do not always exist. We can only hope that this situation will continue to improve. Indeed, even large hospitals and busy practices may not have the right expertise or experience of babies with Down's Syndrome to draw on when new parents ask questions about their particular child. Nor is it an admission of defeat or failure when parents ask for help and advice. Parents are naturally entitled to do the best for their child, and indeed have a responsibility to do so.

Parental rights
As we have seen, under the 1981 and 1988 Education Acts parents have a right by law to have their say on the future of their child's education. A Statement will be made on the child's needs and how they can best be met and provided for. This Statement will be compiled from advice sought from the multi-disciplinary team of professionals who may already be concerned with the child's welfare and development. Any of the following may be involved: the educational psychologist, medical officer, school, speech therapist, social worker or advisory teachers for partially sighted and hearing, indeed anyone who has been working with the child before he starts school. The parents are kept informed throughout this process, their advice is sought, and they have a right to agree or disagree with the statement or provision. Whilst attending school, an annual review of the child's Statement will be held. All professionals involved with the child will be invited together with the (child and) parents to assess the child's progress,

needs and provision. Targets will be set for the coming year.

The curriculum within special educational provision is usually planned towards five major areas of development. Attention will be paid to all the child's individual needs and to its total well-being. The child's needs will be diagnosed and assessed, a suitable programme prepared, taught and evaluated. This is an ongoing process. This provision for all-round development is aimed to increase skills in communication, social competence, physical aptitude, self-help skills and cognitive ability. The child will be able to participate in all kinds of activities to promote these skills and it will be provided with many experiences to develop understanding and ability. Its also has an entitlement and access to the National Curriculum. The child will be able to progress at its own rate, and be encouraged to develop its potential and to become, as far as possible, an independent and responsible young person.

Until recent years the responsibility for children with a learning disability, including Down's Syndrome, lay with the NHS to provide a caring environment. Because of the numbers of 'patients' and limited staff resources available there was usually very little time to devote to teaching and encouraging children to do things for themselves, thus very few persons were able to achieve any measure of independence. Other children were kept at home where they could be looked after by their own family. Attitudes, fashions and terms are now changing. But it is only since 1971 that all children were brought under the education umbrella, and were to receive education according to their needs, even if they were profoundly disabled and receiving care within a hospital situation. Since then the *Warnock Report* on Children with Special Needs was published containing many recommendations, leading to the 1981 Education Act and subsequent Education Acts of 1988 and 1992 and the Code of Practice (Special Educational Needs) in 1994. Children with special needs and learning difficulties should now receive adequate educational provision commensurate with their needs. The modern trend now has an emphasis on integration, both within the school and within the community, rather than segregation as previously.

Given due care and attention and plenty of stimulation, acompanied by a lot of praise and encouragement, the child should continue to progress and develop along recognised and acceptable paths each at its own pace. We should all respond by saying, 'Come and do this like a good boy,' and 'Well, you did try hard, that's good!' – rather than, 'No! Don't do that, it's naughty,' or 'That's not very good, I don't like that.' Reserve the negative attitude for when it is absolutely necessary.

It will probably have more impact! The child is more likely to respond favourably to a positive approach, and will want to please you, in turn. Keep trying anyway. Show that you are pleased with the efforts and that you are happy and love him or her.

Nothing can be more rewarding than to watch a child grow in confidence and self-esteem, happy and busily occupied. You will also get what you expect. If you expect your child to do nothing he may do nothing, or exhibit bad behaviour to get your attention. If you expect your child to achieve, and patiently persist, he will strive towards that aim, a little step at a time.

For the new baby the future lies a long way ahead. In the meantime there is a lot of busy and exciting growing up to be done. Life has to be explored, shared and enjoyed. There are new opportunities opening up all the time. Take courage; go out and find these opportunities and take full advantage of them. Encourage the child in your care to extend his experiences and abilities. Let it discover in life a purpose and a meaning. Let it do things for itself to become fully involved and so have a happy and rewarding life. Today, children with Down's Syndrome are living in a new enlightened age, and are already stepping through this door into a bright new future. They too can grow up secure, confident and happy, prepared to take their place in the community and workplace where they can be socially competent and acceptable. Why not indeed! It is their birthright. The parents and all carers have an all-important role to play to guide them past the milestones, ever constant, praising, supporting and rewarding effort. Even though other means of support may come and go you will still be there; the responsibility is yours. Your child needs you.

Appendix I:
What *is* Down's Syndrome?

The incidence of the birth of a baby with Down's Syndrome is about one in every 1,000, resulting in about 1,000 births each year. The risk can be present at any time, but will frequently relate to the age of the mother, and will increase with maternal age. Under the age of 30 the mother has an initial risk of about 1 in 1,000, where by 45 the chances are as high as 1 in 30. After the age of 45 the risk is generally considered to be too high. The incidence was not previously considered, apparently, to be related to the paternal age, as fresh sperm cells are being continually produced. However, this view now appears to be changing. The risk rises with maternal age, as the egg cells have always been present within the ovaries. It is thought that the older ovum may be more prone to result in an unusual division of chromosomes once it has been fertilised and starts to divide, the chromosomes so producing new cells in the developing foetus.

In 1959 Professor Lejeune in France proved Down's Syndrome to be a genetic condition caused by an etra chromosome. Cells within a 'normal' person contain 46 chromosomes, i.e. 23 pairs. At conception, when the male sperm fertilises the female ovum, 23 chromosomes are inherited from each parent and pair together, resulting in a new set of 46 chromosomes. As the original cells grow and divide, the chromosomes within the cells divide ready to form the new cells. An extra chromosome results when one fails to divide normally, in this instance number 21. The two remain to pair with one other, so producing 3 of the same in the new cell, called **trisomy 21**. Within the dividing cells accidents may also occur producing an unusual, and not a complete, division. When the cells divide and result in trisomy 21 this condition is now known as Down's Syndrome. **Regular trisomy 21**, when all the cells are affected, accounts for some 95 per cent of births with Down's Syndrome.

Sometimes **translocation** may occur; this is an inherited tendency from the maternal ovum or the paternal sperm, which produces an extra chromosome or fragment upon division which can translocate and become attached to another chromosome. This can account for some 3 per cent of all births with Down's Syndrome. Occasionally it may be found that not all the cells contain the extra chromosome, and this condition is known as **mosaic** (about 2–3 per cent of births). A few mothers, with Down's Syndrome themselves, have given birth: some have produced normal babies and some with Down's Syndrome. Medical science is able to describe how this condition occurs but not, as yet, *why* it should happen or why such an imbalance of genetic material should cause such a multiplicity of defects, with a tendency to some mental impairment.

The term Down's Syndrome is now used in preference to 'mongol' (arising from the mongoloid features and now outdated) and is attributed to Professor Down. John Langdon Down was the medical superintendent of Earlswood Asylum for Idiots in Surrey. At the time the terms 'cretin', 'imbecile' and 'idiot' were in use to classify degrees of mental disability and deficiency. In 1866 he wrote a paper entitled *Observations on an Ethnic Classification of Idiots*. The common features which he described are still relevant and used in diagnosis today. He drew attention to the physical features and described other traits, describing their lively sense of the ridiculous, sense of humour, aptitude for mimicry, thick indistinct speech and special liability to winter infections. Interestingly, he also mentioned the gains that will result from efforts of training!

There are several characteristic traits which are common to children with Down's Syndrome, but not all children possess all of the features. Similarly, most of these characteristics may also be found within the so-called normal population, though usually to a lesser degree. Generally speaking, babies with Down's Syndrome may manifest any of the following conditions: low birth weight, flattish faces (and back of the skull), high cheek bones, slanty eyes, sometimes with an epicanthic fold of skin, loose skin at the back of the neck, floppy limbs, lack of muscle tone, difficulty in sucking, short stubby fingers and toes, single (semian) palm crease, large tongue (although this may frequently be of normal size, but the jaw and mouth appear smaller in comparison). They may also be at risk of heart or breathing problems, and sometimes leukaemia or duodenal bowel obstruction. The skin, too, may often contain many peculiarities. There is frequently thick mucous present in the nose (which is usually small); the children tend to be susceptible to frequent colds, catarrh and winter ailments. However, very few normal children survive babyhood without catching some kind of infection, so guard your child's health carefully! Another common feature is the presence of a flattened pelvis so producing a wider angle for the hip joint and ability to extend the leg. They find it effortless to do 'the splits' and frequently find it more comfortable to sit cross-legged.

The incidence of a recurrence of a birth with Down's Syndrome is only about 1 in every 1,000. With increasing age, a mother contemplating another baby will wish to take advice, either by consulting a genetic counsellor, or undertaking a diagnostic or screening test. This is not to be undertaken lightly, since there could be a risk of harming the unborn baby, or the mother herself. It is also a lengthy and complicated procedure. It is usually only undertaken if it is felt that there is indeed a risk involved, and that an abortion will be desired should the result prove positive. The best time to do this is between 16 and 18 weeks of pregnancy. **Routine diagnostic testing** is, at the time of writing, offered to mothers of 35 or over. It is possible that this may become even more widely available. There are three main types of diagnostic tests available and several types of screening tests. Screening is undertaken to assess the likelihood or chances that the mother may have of producing a baby with Down's Syndrome, and at present can only give a low degree of accuracy. If the results indicate the possibility of a positive result a diagnostic test will be offered. These results will be able to prove, to a greater degree of accuracy (almost 100 per cent with amniocentesis), that the baby will have Down's Syndrome.

Amniocentesis is offered routinely to mothers over the age of 35. It is undertaken between 16 and 18 weeks of pregnancy. A needle is inserted into the uterus and a sample of amniotic fluid withdrawn. This fluid will contain cells from the baby which can be grown in a culture and tested for the number of chromosomes present. There is only about 1 per cent inaccuracy and only about 1 per cent risk of danger to mother or baby.

A second type of diagnostic test which can be used is **Chorionic Villus Sampling** (CVS). Ultrasound is used to guide a hollow needle into the uterus and a tiny piece of the placenta (afterbirth) is removed for testing. This can be performed at 10 weeks. A preliminary result may be available within 1 to 3 days, but a more accurate result is available within 3 to 4 weeks.

The third type of diagnostic test which can be used is **Cordocentesis** (fetal blood sampling). This is occasionally offered at 18 weeks with results in one week. A needle is passed through the mother's abdomen and a sample of the baby's blood taken from the umbilical cord for testing.

Screening can only estimate the chances of having a baby with

Down's Syndrome. The process involves taking a blood sample and testing for proteins. Several tests are available. Maternal serum screening will meaure the amounts of protein produced by the developing baby and an assessment will be made in combination with the mother's age, weight and length of pregnancy to estimate the chance. Usually, if the chances are more than 1 in 250, this will produce a screen positive result and an amniocentesis is offered and then a choice to continue or terminate the pregnancy. A screen negative result of 1 in 250 indicates that the chances are unlikely.

Alpha Fetoprotein (AFP) is one kind of protein produced by all developing babies. Some hospitals use low levels of AFP testing for screening. Only about 30 per cent of babies with Down's Syndrome are detected. At present this has a high rate of false positive results.

The **Triple Test** measures three proteins: AFP, unconjugated oestriol (uE3) and human chorionic gonodothropin (hCG) in one blood sample. This can produce a positive screen for about 60 per cent of babies with Down's Syndrome. In some instances a **Double Test** or **Triple Plus Test** may be offered. High resolution ultrasound scans in some hospitals may give an indication, but no definite diagnosis.

The risk of producing a second child with Down's Syndrome can be greater. Blood tests and ultrasound screening can only estimate. Diagnostic tests will provide a greater degree of accuracy. If parents feel at risk, before pregnancy, during preg- nancy or following the birth of a baby with Down's Syndrome, they can seek the advice of a genetic counsellor who can be contacted through the hospital, paediatrician or child development centre. The genetic counsellor will be able to explain any risk or implications.

Your baby may present many problems of one kind or another as he grows into childhood and beyond – but, then, so will any baby, as most will meet minor ailments and complaints to overcome. It is a part of normal childhood and development! Given adequate stimulation and attention there appears to be no reason today why any child with Down's Syndrome should not be able to lead a relatively normal, happy and rewarding life.

Increasingly more and more children with Down's Syndrome are receiving full-time education within our mainstream schools with an entitlement to the National Curriculum, and obtaining jobs in the community.

Appendix II:
An Historical Overview

1866 Dr John Langdon Down classified characteristics commonly shared by people with Down's Syndrome.

1944 Education Act was designed to provide 'education for all' according to age, ability and aptitude, but with some exceptions including children who were 'ineducable' (i.e. mentally handicapped =learning disabilities).

1946 Mencap (Royal Society for Mentally Handicapped Children and Adults) was formed. The Society aims to improve the quality of life for people with learning disabilities, and raise the level of public awareness. It should be noted that mental handicap is not to be confused with mental illness.

1970 Down's Babies Association was formed. This became in . . .

1976 The Down's Children Association and then in . . .

1986 Down's Syndrome Association (DSA). The Down's Syndrome Association offers help and support to families and carers of people with Down's Syndrome and the professionals who work with them and works to promote positive public attitudes.

1970 Education Act legally entitled all children to receive education. This included those who were formerly 'ineducable' and who were in the care of the NHS.

1978 *Warnock Report* summarised current thinking at the time on all aspects of special needs through from pre-school to post-school provision. It contained over 200 recommendations including replacing 'labels' with a Statement of special needs, integration, parental rights and the responsibility of the school to identify special needs. It identified 2 per cent of children as needing special educational provision throughout their school life and a further 18 per cent as needing special educational provision at some time during their school life (as many as 1 in 5 at any given time). Many of the recommendations became law in the . . .

1981 Education Act which asserted the right for children with special educational needs to be educated alongside their peers in a mainstream school. It defined children with Special Educational Needs as those who required additional or different provision from that 'made generally' within the local education authority, and required the LEA to provide Statements of Special Educational Needs.

1988 Education Act introduced a National Curriculum and local management of schools (LMS) with barely any reference to furthering or maintaining the provision of Special Educational Needs.

1989 The Children Act defined responsibilities and rights for children who are in care.

1992 Education Act superseded the previous Acts. Schools are to provide information on how they meet the Special Educational Needs of their pupils.

1994 Code of Practice set out in detail the procedures for Statementing in school to a five-point plan, the role of the Special Needs Coordinator (SENCO) and the setting of targets at the annual review of the Statement.

Selected Reading List

A Benefits Guide for Children and Young People with Disabilities, Bernie Graham and Nigel Pegram (Disability Alliance, ERA, 1992).

Caught in the Act – Children with Special Needs – Assessment, Law and Practice, Harry Chasty and John Friel (Jessica Kingsley, 1993).

Children With Special Needs, Richard Woolfson (Faber and Faber, 1991).

Current Approaches to Down's Syndrome, David Lane and Brian Stratford (eds.) (Holt Reinhart and Winston, 1985).

Disability Rights Handbook, Sally Robertson (Disability Alliance, ERA, 1994).

Down's Syndrome, Dr Richard Newton (Optima, 1992).

Down's Syndrome – Moving Through Life, Yvonne Burns and Pat Gunn (Chapman and Hall, 1993).

Down's Syndrome – Past, Present and Future, Brian Stratford (Penguin, 1989).

Down's Syndrome. The Facts, Mark Seilkowitch (Oxford University Press, 1990).

How to Claim State Benefits Martin Rathfelder (How to Books, 1995).

I'm Louise, Anne Rooke (LDA, Cambs., 1986).

Let Me Play, Dorothy Jeffree, Roy McConkey and Simon Hewson (Souvenir Press, 1994).

Play Helps, Roma Lear (Butterworth-Heinemann, 1993).

Reading and Language Development in Children with Down's Syndrome, Sue Buckley (Portsmouth Down's Syndrome Trust, 1984).

The Adolescent with Down's Syndrome: Life for the Teenager and the Family, S. Buckley and R. Sachs (Portsmouth Down's Syndrome Trust, 1987).

The Children Act (Mencap, 1992).

Two Words together Bill Gillam (George Allen and Unwin, 1983).

Will my Son, Sarah Boston (Pluto Press, 1980).

Your Baby Has Down's Syndrome (DSA, free to new parents).

Useful Addresses

Disabled Living Foundation, 380–384 Harrow Road, London W9 2H4. Tel: (0171) 289 6111.

Down's Syndrome Association, 155 Mitcham Road, London SW17 9PG. Tel: (0181) 682 4001.

Down's Syndrome Screening Service, Institute of Epidemiology and Health Services Research, 34 Hyde Terrace, Leeds LS2 9NL. Tel: (0113) 234 4013.

Early Learning Centre, Havelock, Hawksworth, Swindon, Wiltshire. Tel: (01793) 831300.

Home Farm Trust Ltd, 54 Queen Square, Bristol BS1 4LH. Tel: (0117) 927 3746.

King's Fund Centre, 126 Albert Street, London NW1 7NP. Tel: (0171) 267 6111.

Learning Development Aids, Duke Street, Wisbech, Cambridgeshire PE13 2AE. Tel: (01945) 63441.

Makaton Vocabulary Development Project, 31 Firwood Drive, Camberley, Surrey. Tel: (01276) 61390.

Mencap, 123 Golden Lane, London EC1Y 0RT. Tel: (0171) 454 0454.

Portage, NFER Nelson, Darville House, 2 Oxford Road East, Windsor, Berkshire SL4 1DF. Tel: (01753) 574123.

Portsmouth Down's Syndrome Trust, Portsmouth University, King Charles Street, Portsmouth, Hampshire PO1 2EP. Tel: (01705) 824261.

Rex Brinkworth (contact via the Down's Syndrome Association).

SKILL (National Bureau for Students with Disabilities), 336 Brixton Road, London SW9 7AA. Tel: (0171) 274 0565.

Voluntary Council for Handicapped Children, 8 Wakeley Street, London EC1V 7QE. Tel: (0171) 278 9441.

Index

More *Resources in Education* Titles from Northcote House

The following pages contain details of a selection of other titles from the *Resources in Education* series. For further information, and details of our Inspection Copy Service, please apply to:

Northcote House Publishers Ltd, Plymbridge House, Estover Road, Plymouth PL6 7PY, United Kingdom. Tel: Plymouth (01752) 202301. Fax: (01752) 202330.

A selection of catalogues and brochures is usually available on request.

Beyond the Core Curriculum
Co-Ordinating the Other Foundation Subjects in Primary Schools

EDITED BY
MIKE HARRISON

To help schools to meet the needs of the National Curriculum, primary teachers are required increasingly to act as consultants to their colleagues in particular subjects. This task of curriculum co-ordination often demands a new range of skills from teachers whose expertise may, hitherto, have been confined mainly to classroom teaching.

This practical book helps those charged with leading their school's staff in: Geography, History, Physical Education, Information Technology, Music, Art and Design, Technology, and Religious Education to develop their subject knowledge, network with others and find ways to influence colleagues to ensure that their subject is taught imaginatively and coherently in the school.

Written by a team of primary specialists this book offers invaluable advice and support to headteachers, teachers and students for whom the co-ordination of the foundation subjects in primary schools is an area of growing interest and responsibility.

The Editor, Mike Harrison, is Director of the Centre for Primary Education in the University of Manchester. He has worked as a primary teacher and a headteacher, leads primary pre-service education and is currently running inter-LEA courses for primary co-ordinators. He is known nationally for his courses on education management for prospective primary deputy heads. He is co-author of *Primary School Management* (Heinemann, 1992).

The ten co-authors are all primary experts in their fields, many running twenty-day training courses for primary co-ordinators in their subjects.

Paperback, 192 pages, tables., 0-7463-0649-0

The Language of Discipline

A practical approach to effective classroom management

Second Edition

BILL ROGERS

All teachers at some point in their careers encounter discipline problems in the classroom. Newly qualified and trainee teachers, in particular, often find classroom control the most demanding aspect of their new profession.

In this highly practical and user-friendly handbook Bill Rogers shows, step-by-step, how to draw up an effective discipline plan and strike the right balance between encouragement and correction. Good discipline does not just happen but is the product of careful planning, behaviour analysis, and the appropriate use of language and assertive skills. This book addresses all forms of disruptive behaviour, especially hostile and argumentative students, and shows that it is possible for every teacher, however inexperienced, to establish effective control and provide the right learning environment for the entire class. It will be welcomed by all teachers seeking a long-term positive solution to the demanding problem of disruptive behaviour in the classroom.

Bill Rogers is an education consultant specialising in classroom discipline and management, and teacher peer support. He was consultant to the *Elton Report: Discipline in Schools* (1989) and to the Victoria Ministry of Education (1985–88). He has taught at every level of education and written many articles and several books on discipline, teacher stress and teacher welfare including: *You Know the Fair Rule* (Longman, 1991), *Supporting Teachers in the Workplace* (Jacaranda, 1992), and *Making a Discipline Plan* (Nelson, 1989). He now lectures and runs INSET course in Australia and the United Kingdom where he is attached annually to the University of Cambridge Institute of Education to run in-service programmes on discipline and peer support for teachers.

Paperback, 176 pages, tables, 0-7463-0862-0

Managing Stress in Schools
A practical guide to effective strategies for teachers

MARIE BROWN & SUE RALPH

Managing stress is a growing problem for teachers in schools as they seek to meet the increasing demands of the National Curriculum, local management of schools (LMS), and the rising expectations of parents understandably wanting quantifiable examination results for their children approaching the highly competitive labour or higher education markets for the first time.

Based on sound psychological theory and research the emphasis of this book is, throughout, on practical solutions to teacher stress. Its sound analysis and realistic advice will enable teachers and those responsible for staff development both to identify the causes of stress, and to formulate a whole school policy for its management within the school.

Sue Ralph and Marie Brown both teach in the University of Manchester School of Education. They lecture and research in Educational Management and Administration, and Education and the Mass Media, and run inservice courses for teachers and other professionals. They have researched and published extensively on the effects of stress on teachers.

Paperback, 128 pages, tables. 0-7463-0652-0

Managing the
Primary School Budget

BRENT DAVIES & LINDA ELLISON

With the framework of the Local Management of Schools firmly in place, heads, staff and governors need to turn their attention to its implementation at the local school level.

This practical guide begins by establishing the key dimensions of LMS and reviews the nature of income and expenditure in the primary school. It moves on to a consideration of the way in which budgeting fits into school management development planning and examines the role of staff and governors in the process.

The book then adopts a step-by-step approach using a case study school to demonstrate how to go through the three key stages of budgetary review, planning and implementation. This will provide primary schools with a practical framework enabling them to manage their new-found financial responsibilities.

Brent Davies BA MSc is Director of the International Educational Leadership and Management Centre, University of Humberside and is an LMS adviser to a large number of local education authorities. He has provided LMS management training for over 1000 primary heads in differing LEAs. He is the author of *Local Management of Schools* and a large number of articles on delegated finance. He is joint author with Linda Ellison of *Education Management for the 1990s*.

Linda Ellison MSc is a Senior Lecturer in charge of Education Management at Leeds Metropolitan University. She is extensively involved with programmes of senior management training, particularly for heads and deputies in primary schools. She has also been involved in the provision of staff development on LMS in a variety of LEAs. She is joint author with Brent Davies of *Education Management for the 1990s*.

Paperback, 128 pages, tables, 0-7463-0592-3

Marketing the Primary School
An Introduction for Teachers and Governors

BRIAN HARDIE

Schools have always had an eye on their 'reputation' and standing within the local community. However, open enrolment and competition for pupil numbers following the 1988 Education Reform Act have put a much greater value on the relationship which schools need to have with both parents and pupils. Now, in order to increase — and even maintain — pupil numbers, schools will be under much greater pressure to market themselves effectively. The author, who has been running courses in marketing and reputation management for primary school heads, shows how the primary school can be successfully promoted, stretching precious resources to make the most of contacts with the local community. Contents: Preface, the school in its marketplace, reputation management, marketing the school, meeting the customer, the prospectus and other communications, handling the media, further reading, useful addresses, glossary, index.

Brian Hardie MA DLC is an Education Consultant and formerly Senior Lecturer in Education Management at Crewe + Alsager Faculty of the Metropolitan University of Manchester, where he ran courses in marketing and reputation management for primary school Heads. He is the author of *Evaluating the Primary School* (Northcote House, 1994).

'...tells head how to think the unthinkable... sound advice about things that good schools should have been doing for years...' *Times Educational Supplement.*

'The book works, as a handbook to be used and returned to as different activities are needed. The context and priority are right... the ingredients for the successful mix are right... the focus and presentation of the advice are simple and sharp.' *NAGM News.*

Paperback, 144 pages, illustrated, 0-7463-0591-5

Local Management of Schools

BRENT DAVIES & CHRIS BRAUND

Written by two consultants in this important field, this book meets the pressing need for an introductory handbook to help governors, teachers and parents get to grips with major new responsibilities now becoming mandatory. Readable and practical, the book spells out the new legislation and what it means, the new financial structure in secondary and primary schools, the new role of Head teachers and governors in delegated school management, and what it means for the future. Complete with case studies and suggested management exercises.

'The nine main chapters, each dealing with a different aspect, are easy to read, comparatively jargon-free, and gave me a very good overview of LMS.... This reference book will justify a place in any educational establishment because of its accessible information and advice.' *Junior Education*. 'Well favoured by the brevity/practicality formula, written with governors and parents in mind as well as teachers. It is strong on illustrative yet simple graphics and tables and does not shirk the consequences of falling numbers.' *Times Educational Supplement*.

Paperback, 96 pages, tables, 0-7463-0574-5

The School Library

ELIZABETH KING MA ALA

Written by a former Chairperson of the School Library Association, this book appraises the role of school libraries in a changing world — a world in which new ideas, new technology and new initiatives (and financial cutbacks) present a special challenge for the professional. 'A stimulating appraisal of the role of the school library in a changing educational world of cutbacks, information technology and educational reform.' *Junior & Middle School Education Journal*.

Paperback, 112 pages, illustrated. 0-7463-0517-6

The School Meals Service

NAN BERGER OBE FHCIMA

The importance of the school meals service is becoming better recognised today, following greater interest in diet and health, and the advent of privatisation and what it means for standards of service in the educational system. This new book meets the longstanding need for an introduction to—and defence of—the School Meals Service. Expert, readable and forthright, it reviews key health and management issues for everyone having a professional interest in children's welfare, from head teachers and governors to catering managers and educational administrators.

Contents: Foreword, acknowledgements, the beginnings, what the service is and does, the structure of the service, training, nutrition, organising the production of school meals, the stigma of the free school meal, the competition, the problem of midday supervision, the economics of the School Meals Service, the effects of the Education (No. 2) Act 1980, the role of the Government, the future of the School Meals Service, appendices (organisations, statistics, notes on Scotland and Northern Ireland), chronology, bibliography, index.

'Informative, thought-provoking and controversial.' *Lunch Times*. 'Maori-style cooking has not, to my knowledge, been much practised by our own School Meals Service, though no doubt ungrateful children would have their parents believe otherwise. The kind of folklore perception of school dinners is tackled in Nan Berger's School Meals Service. There is much more to the book than this, however, for it is a thorough and well documented history of the meals service, starting with its origins in the last century and moving on to recent traumas of privatisation and closure.' *Times Educational Supplement*. Nan Berger OBE FHCIMA is former Editor of the *National Association of School Meals Organisers Handbook* and *Hospitality* magazine.

Paperback, 144 pages, illustrated, 0-7463-0518-4

Adventure in Education
Team building through outdoor pursuits

Adventure in Education is a practical collection of team building games, ideas and initiative tasks which can be used individually or as the core of a complete team building programme. Each task is easily employed and explained in detail with all the necessary information, diagrams, cartoon-type illustrations and photographs together with suggested progressions as the group's skills develop,

All the activities have been extensively group tested to provide a positive approach to social learning through team activity but without the competitive underpinning, or indeed the need to teach and learn ball skills, which invariably slow down the process.

This is a whole new ball game. No ball. No losers. Everyone wins.

Richard Andrews is a teacher of PE and Drama in a Secondary school in Kent. He developed the material in this book over many years of working with young people after perceiving a need for a range of activities to develop their social and physical skills in an enjoyable way regardless of sporting ability.

Paperback, 112 pages, illustrated, 0-7564-0682-2

School Development Planning
A practical guide to the strategic management process

This practical handbook explains clearly the role of planning and OFSTED in recent educational reforms and details the strategic importance of school development planning in improving the quality and increasing the effectiveness of a school and its management. Written by an experienced school manager and senior lecturer in education management this book provides a step-by-step guide to the planning process, describes in detail how to produce a plan that works and, by means of a full case study, explores and advises on ways of avoiding the common pitfalls of the planning process. It will be an invaluable source of information and guidance to all those involved in planning for a school's future or preparing for an OFSTED inspection

Corrie Giles BEd, MSc, Cert. Ed, taught and held senior management positions in comprehensive schools for 17 years before becoming Senior Lecturer in Education Management at Manchester Metropolitan University. Currently he is a consultant in education management in Canada where he teaches on the MEd programme at an Ontario university. He maintains academic links in the UK through consultancy work and university teaching.

Paperback, 128 pages, charts and tables, 0-7463-0626-1